# Back to the Bundu

03 May 2014

Ray,

I'm glad you enjoyed reading about my adventures in South Africa and Botswana!

## ALSO BY MATT ARTZ

*Down to Africa*

*The Stone Apocalypse*

*A Life Outside*

*A Life Outside 2*

*Boulderfest!*

# Back to the Bundu

Adventures in Botswana's Tuli Wilderness

By Matt Artz

First Edition, May 2013

ISBN 978-1-304-00854-1

*For Ruth,*

*who was born in Africa,*

*but moved away at about 6 months of age,*

*and thus has no memories of this fascinating continent.*

*I'll take you back there someday, my love.*

*But not like this…*

# Acknowledgements

A deep and heartfelt thank you to all of the wonderful and special people who made my adventures in Botswana and South Africa so memorable, including Lisa, Anneline, Gabbi, Ruby, William, Edward, Christoff, Bethule, Johann, Jocelyn, Martin, and especially Johannes, Ash, and Andrew. You made me feel welcome, you made me feel at home, and you taught me about your way of life. I'll never forget.

Thanks also to Ruth, David, Mike, Tom, Rob, and all of the others who read and reviewed various drafts of the stories in this book.

Special thanks to my wife, Ruth. She never questioned my desire to go back down to Africa without her; in fact, she encouraged it, because she knew how important it was to me.

# Contents

# Welcome Home

A massive monsoon was churning out in the Indian Ocean between Mozambique and Madagascar. While it was bringing torrential rains to South Africa's Eastern Cape, we didn't expect to get much if any rain from it in eastern Botswana's Tuli Wilderness. It was, however, bringing us a truly oppressive blend of heat and humidity that was impossible to escape—so much so that we delayed the start time for our afternoon game drive from 4 to 5 p.m. with the hope that it might cool down even just a little bit.

When we started off in the Land Rover a little after 5, the heat was still unbearable, but the slight breeze that came from sitting in the open, moving vehicle was a welcome relief. Martin, director of the African Conservation Experience (ACE) program, was taking a group of nine university students from the UK out on their last game drive before they headed back home, and invited me along to sit in the passenger seat of the vehicle. Out in front, in the tracking seat—a small jump seat bolted to the hood of the vehicle, so that when you sit in it your feet are literally hanging out in front of the bumper—was Johannes (or "Oboss"), a San Bushman who was an expert tracker, one of the best in the world, carrying 1,000 years of tracking experience in his 70-something-year-old body. He also had six-pack abs that any 25-year-old would die for.

Our first wildlife sighting that evening was a pair of ostrich—not the most exciting thing for me, having just come from the Polokwane Game Reserve in South Africa where I saw dozens of the large, awkward birds traipsing across the landscape. And these two looked thin and scraggly compared to those in

1

Polokwane, thanks no doubt to the harsh, unforgiving landscape of the Tuli Wilderness. Five minutes later, Johannes spotted a lone steenbock high on a ridge, framed beautifully by the slightly cloudy evening skies. I then spotted a second steenbock running across the same ridge, spooked by our presence, although we were at least a quarter of a mile away and 300 feet below it.

Just as I was starting to get a feel for what I thought it was going to be like in the Tuli Wilderness—driving long distances on terribly rutted roads to see a few animals scattered here and there struggling for a meager existence in this fragile and truly wild landscape—we stumbled across our first herd of elephants.

-----

Johannes saw them first, of course, and Martin quickly and deftly turned the Land Rover to the right, onto a barely perceptible dirt track through the tall grass leading directly towards the herd. He turned off the motor while we were still moving and coasted silently down the gentle grade, gradually losing speed, and with the last few seconds of inertia on his side he turned off of the faint path and went sideways into the virgin grass, coming to a stop at the perfect angle for us to watch the herd cross the road a few hundred feet in front of us.

We sat there for about 15 minutes or more, watching the herd move slowly past us in the waning light, pulling up large tufts of green grass with their trunks, shaking them back and forth to remove the dirt attached to the roots, and then placing them in their mouths to chew. We watched in near total silence, except for the crunching sounds of the elephants eating, and their occasional grunting.  As the last in line, the massive bull male, crossed the rough dirt track to rejoin his herd, Johannes counted a total of 34 elephants in this group.

When they had moved a sufficient distance away, Martin restarted the Land Rover and we moved on further towards our intended destination—the Motloutse River, which still had a little bit of water left in it this late in the rainy season, and where we hoped to see more elephants and other animals coming down to take one last long, deep drink before the night came.

As we got closer to the river, the monsoonal winds started to pick up, eventually getting quite strong, bringing a cool relief to us humans but casting an unusual sense of foreboding on this serene landscape.  We saw no elephants or other animals down at the river, but still enjoyed our short time there—the evening sun reflecting off of the thin ribbons of water in the sandy riverbed; the sand bars punctured seemingly everywhere by large circular depressions (elephant footprints); and the high river bank littered with heavy debris from the devastating floods that had swept through this region just a month earlier.  But it was getting dark, it was almost time for dinner, and the winds were really starting to blow.  It was time to go.

-----

As we drove back towards camp, my eyes stung from the persistent red dust being kicked up by the vehicle and the monsoonal winds ("Tuli" means "dust" in the Setswana language).  Then we spotted a second large herd of elephants just ahead and off to our right, this one even closer to us than the first herd.  Rather than slow down and stop to watch them, this time Martin accelerated to move past them as quickly as

3

possible—and not just because we were late for dinner. "This wind really agitates them," he said, "and I'd hate for us to get trapped between a herd of elephants and the river in this kind of wind." Five or ten years ago it was said that the elephants of the greater Tuli area were easily the most aggressive elephants in all of Africa, and although they've since calmed down a bit and become slightly more comfortable around humans, all it might take is a little thing like a strong wind to get them agitated and regressing back to their aggressive state.

About a mile further, we approached a sharp bend in the road near one of a few large clumps of trees left in this part of the Tuli Wilderness (most trees here looking more like shrubs, having long ago been chomped and chewed down by the more than 1,300 elephants that roam freely through the greater Tuli area). The sharp turn was made even more precarious by the fading light, almost completely gone now.

As we approached the blind turn, Martin slowed the vehicle, and we suddenly found ourselves practically face-to-face with a large, dark, looming object just 20 to 30 feet away.

It was a juvenile male elephant, not quite a baby, but not quite old enough to be on its own just yet. We startled him as much as he startled us, and he took off running fast to the left, lifting his trunk high and trumpeting loudly. This was a signal to his mother, who was no doubt nearby, and who was already on edge because of the winds; now somebody was messing with her little boy.

"I don't like this," Martin said. "This is exactly the situation I didn't want to be in."

We all started scanning the brush to the right, where the elephant had come from, and where presumably the rest of the herd was, looking for more large looming shapes in the twilight which might decide to charge us. Huge termite mounds and clumps of dead brush behind green bushes tricked our eyes in the fading light, and several times we imagined we saw mom on her way to save her baby boy and/or destroy our vehicle. Martin continuously moved the Land Rover forward 10 yards, then backwards 10 yards, then forward 10 yards again. At one point he reached up to the rifle case attached to the edge of the hood and unzipped it, preparing for a quick response in the worst case scenario. One of the students behind me whispered "Oh, shit!" In their two weeks out in the bush with Martin, they had never seen him this flustered.

We continued forward and eventually found the rest of the herd off to the right about 100 yards ahead. The mother was looking intently at us, watching our every move, her trunk held high in the air ahead of her, sniffing at the air for any signs of danger, her nostrils unable to make sense of anything in the strong wind. With the elephants at our back but seemingly now out of danger, Martin put the Land Rover in four-wheel drive mode and we dropped into a steep, narrow, seemingly impassable ravine, and then we quickly shot up the other side. "You can see that if they had come after us, this crossing would have been the absolute worst possible place for us to be," he said.

But they didn't come after us. They just continued to graze in the heavy grass, the adolescent one off on his own trying to figure out how to rejoin his herd, while the humans that scared him were heading back to camp for a hearty dinner.

-----

About twenty minutes later, at a steep, rough spot called "Horrible Hill" on the dirt road back to camp, we were climbing slowly but steadily up the rocky path when a loud hissing sound abruptly came from underneath the engine. It only lasted a second or two, but Martin didn't like what he had heard, so he turned off the motor. Johannes did a quick inspection by flashlight and let us know that there was a large puddle of oil on the ground underneath the vehicle. Apparently this Land Rover had recently had a new engine installed, but that new engine had a bad habit of blowing out the oil seal.

Martin radioed back to camp to request a rescue vehicle to come and evacuate us. We all stood around in the dark, talking about what we had just experienced on the drive, and listening to the sounds of the African night. Twenty minutes later, two vehicles arrived to load us all up and take us back to camp, where a welcome, if slightly cold meal was waiting for us.

And that was just my first of more than 20 game drives and walks in the Tuli Wilderness of Botswana.

It got even better from there.

# Returning to a Place I've Never Been

Sitting in the passenger seat of the open Land Rover, speeding across the open plains of southern Africa as the sun was setting, my expert guide Martin turned to me and asked, "So, Matt, what is it that you do to keep bread on the table?"

"I work for a software company," I replied and, feeling more than a little envious of his lifestyle and cynical about my own, added "I work in an office all day."

"Wow, that's very different than this," he replied.

After a long pause he looked me in the eye and added, "It's hard for me to even comprehend what you do every day."

Yeah, dude. Tell me about it.

It wasn't supposed to be like this. How exactly did I get here? No, not how did I end up with Martin in a Land Rover moving across the wild grasslands of eastern Botswana looking for herds of Africa elephants; but how in the hell did I end up stuck in a windowless office staring at a computer screen for 8 to 10 hours a day and calling that a life?

It's a long story, and it's not really what this book is about. But suffice it to say that, over the years, I made many decisions based on a quest for "stability" and doing the "right" thing and what was "expected." I regret nothing, and in hindsight would most likely make all of the same decisions over again. But in the end, by giving up one lifestyle for another, I gave up a little bit of what makes me tick as a human being; I sacrificed some of life's "grand adventures" for what I call "little adventures" — weekend and other relatively short trips here and there designed to partially quench the desire for wildness, but which in the end just left me thirsty for something more substantial.

I had just turned 50. It was time to set aside the "little adventures" and go on a "grand adventure" for the first time in a long time; to go someplace familiar, yet where I had never been before, and to stay there long enough to drink in every last drop.

-----

Looking back at my childhood, I loved digging holes. Any excuse would do, but an excuse wasn't even necessary.

I remember setting a huge goal for myself one summer vacation in third or fourth grade: I would dig a hole to China. My imagination ran wild with visions of breaking through on the other side of the world and being greeted enthusiastically by people wearing funny hats and holding chopsticks.

It was a lot of work, digging all the way to China, and I gave up after the hole was only about four feet deep. If I had managed to do the impossible and pass through the center of the earth and break through the other side, ironically I would not have found myself standing next to the Great Wall of China or anywhere near it; my exit point would in fact have been much closer to southern Africa, which was literally the other side of the world from where I lived in California.

I eventually made it to the other side of the world. But not by digging.

-----

In January 1976, I moved to South Africa. I was 13 years old. It was my first time out of the United States. It was my first time on an airplane. But it wasn't my first time moving away from home: for as long as I could remember, we had been moving, from one southern California suburb to the next. Changing schools and having to make new friends was always difficult. But this was different. I was moving halfway around the planet, to a strange, foreign land.

My apprehension was tempered by excitement. After all, this wasn't just another cookie-cutter southern California suburb we were moving to; it was Africa. I yearned for it to be an amazing, unforgettable, grand adventure.

And it was.

I saw large, wild animals in their native habitat. I spent countless hours wandering through the brush and grasslands by myself. I entered high school, made new friends, and attempted to learn a new language. I experienced riots, unthinkable repression, and even war. I hiked across the stunning grassy plains and tasted some of the best that Africa had to offer.

My move to South Africa took place more than 35 years ago. I think about my time there frequently, reliving the unforgettable experiences of my adolescence. But only recently was I able to put all of those experiences into context. Although I only lived there for a short time, it happened during an important stage: my transition from child to adult. In many ways, Africa changed me, and Africa made me who I am today.

-----

When we first moved to South Africa in 1976, the country had only just recently entered into the television age. There was only one channel, which broadcast for just a few hours each evening, and everything was broadcast in black-and-white. When the single station started the broadcast "day" around dinner time, it featured a roundup of local and world news, typically followed by re-runs of some horrible old American series I had never heard of, and then a movie before signing off for the evening.

As you can imagine, South Africans were elated to finally enter the modern television era. Not so much for me, though. I was used to watching TV for many hours a day, even if it was just serving as a sort of white noise generator in the background. I was also used to having the option of selecting between many different shows on many different channels. How was I going to survive in this strange land? What would I do with all of this new found free time?

I read books. I read a lot of books.

Perhaps the most uniquely original book—or more accurately, series of books—I read while there carried the promising title of *Bundu Book*. In South African and Rhodesian (Zimbabwean) slang, "bundu" means a wild, desolate region far from human habitation. It comes from the Bantu word for wilderness or a remote, wild place. Published in Rhodesia (now Zimbabwe) in the 1960s and 1970s, the *Bundu Books* were an early, local take on the type of naturalist guides which later became popular as the world embraced the environmental ethic and gained a deeper appreciation of the natural world.

My final memory of South Africa in 1978 is of looking out of the window at the airport in Johannesburg, watching the airplanes taxi on the runway. The sun was setting, casting an eerie pinkish glow unlike any I have ever seen anywhere else in the world except down in southern Africa. I spent my 16th birthday on an airplane travelling from Johannesburg to Nairobi, Kenya, and then on to Zurich, Switzerland before eventually landing in my new home: Athens, Greece. I wondered if I would ever get the opportunity to get back down to Africa, although for many years I honestly didn't spend too much time thinking about it. But it was a feeling that was always there, festering somewhere deep down in the dark recesses of my soul. I didn't realize it for a long time, but it would eventually boil and rise up to the surface. It just took 12,637 days for it to come to a complete boil.

My complete set of *Bundu Books* still sits on my bookshelf at home. They are a reminder of the time I spent down in Africa, and it's easy to see how the content of these books both fostered my interests in many aspects of the natural environment and had a profound influence on the person I am today. I sincerely cherish my complete set of *Bundu Books*, and as the years passed they triggered more and more memories that made me increasingly sentimental, until I longed for the day I could return to southern Africa and once again use the knowledge they contained as I continued my adventures there.

I had to get back to the bundu.

-----

Is it possible to return to a place you've never been before?

When salmon return from years at sea to the stream they were born in, they identify the unique chemical signature of the stream through taste and smell. Like the salmon returning to its mother stream, the taste and smell of Africa was embedded deeply in my unconscious. It was calling me back.

-----

In February 2010, I got called into a meeting with the legendary Jane Goodall to discuss a new community-centered conservation approach that the Jane Goodall Institute had pioneered in their work to save chimpanzees in Tanzania, and how we could all work together to document this approach and apply it to a variety of conservation issues in other parts of the world. There was some concern about how an approach that was started in a small corner of Africa might be applied to the entire world. Just then, Jane, who up to that point had not said a single word in the meeting, spoke up:

"Remember, man himself started in Africa..."

She was right. Everyone originally came from Africa. The rest is just timing. The timing of their migration is just details.

At some point, like a pilgrimage to Mecca, every human being should return to Africa, the original homeland of all humanity.

And later, after reading so much of Jane's first-hand observations of her time in Africa, for the first time in a long time, I really wanted to go back.

-----

On my 40th birthday, I went kayaking up in the San Bernardino Mountains, by myself, at dawn, on a placid lake. Meditating on this milestone, I realized that I had been rushing around for all of my 40 years, in hyperactive mode, trying to do and accomplish as much as humanly possible. Out on the lake that morning in 2002, I made a vow to myself to slow down, and to find enjoyment in the little things. My life up to that point had always been about rushing to the destination. My new mantra became: slow down; enjoy the journey.

I recently celebrated my 50th birthday. A milestone, for sure. If, with a little luck and a heavy dose of modern health care and pharmaceuticals, I am able to do as science is predicting and live to be a hundred years old, this meant that my life was now officially half over. To pay homage to half of my life being gone, I did something uncharacteristically self-indulgent.

For my 50th birthday, I decided to take the ultimate adventure. I would finally go back to Africa. And enjoy not just the experience, but also the journey.

-----            .

Where does the time go? When we get caught up in the days, the hours, and the minutes, the years just seem to fly by. The seemingly endless cycle of school, work, responsibilities—life— make us slaves to the grind. Each year passes more quickly than the previous, and then one day you wake up and realize that too many years have passed in a gigantic blur.

That day for me wasn't an actual day. A series of small events in various segments of my life merged and coagulated, bubbling to the surface to eventually form a big realization.

The world around us is a complex place, and one way we manage that complexity is through a process of abstraction. In its purest sense, abstraction is a reduction of detail down to the bare essentials we still need in order to understand something. Abstraction helps us to simplify things, letting us focus on the information that's most important for the task at hand without sacrificing comprehension—and often even improving it. Removing extraneous elements helps us to cope with complexity. Think of a short story told to teach an important lesson; a simple diagram drawn to explain a complex system; or an elegant map created to demystify a confusing landscape.

Of course, the down side of abstraction is that the more abstract you make something, the more you are removed from the actual thing. Think of it in terms of an airplane flying over the landscape. The closer you are to the ground—the closer you are to reality—the more detail you can see. As the airplane gradually moves higher, you get very different views of the landscape. You see different things when you can see the "big picture," but as your altitude increases you lose more and more detail. It's the paradox of abstraction.

My long fascination with the natural environment reached somewhat of a pinnacle back in the late 1980s in the East Mojave Desert while doing field research for my masters' degree in environmental studies. My thesis topic was studying the impacts of human activities such as roads, pipelines, and electrical lines on desert vegetation. Unfortunately, graduating on my somewhat unrealistic self-imposed timeline required that my field work be done mostly in the brutal summer heat.

Through the generous help of my friends Mike and Marc, my cousin Jeff, and of course my wife Ruth, I was able to complete all of the field work in time to finish my thesis and graduate on time, and all it cost me was money for gas, ice chests full of Gatorade, a few meals of greasy burgers at the famous Bun Boy in the nearby town of Baker, and a few side-trips to make our time out there in the blast furnace of the Mojave more interesting.

After our daily tedium of setting up transects in various locations and measuring and counting creosote, saltbush, and other plants, we traveled widely within the boundaries of what was then called the East Mojave National Scenic Area. We examined ancient Native American petroglyphs etched in the boulders thousands of years ago, explored washes and canyons and the nearby Granite Mountains, walked through a huge Joshua tree forest more densely vegetated than anything that Joshua Tree National Park had to offer, and imagined an earlier California at the old Kelso railway depot. But getting down in the desert dirt and physically touching the creosote bushes and desert saltbush more than anything gave me a detailed understanding and appreciation for this fascinating ecosystem.

Then life got complicated.

Successful completion of my masters' degree quickly led to a full-time job as an environmental scientist. At first, there was some field work involved, which I enjoyed greatly. Over time, as my skills at project management and report writing evolved, the opportunities for hands-on work in the field evaporated like water in the dry Mojave heat.

There were many highlights to this job: travelling around the country assessing the environmental impact destroying the large chemical weapons stockpiles the US still had on hand from the Cold War; using cutting-edge computer models to calculate the noise and air pollution impacts from new highway projects across the US and new airport projects across the globe; leading my first projects for NASA/JPL's Goldstone Deep Space Communications Complex (and as part of this project getting to land and take off in a NASA plane on the runway at Edwards Air Force Base where the Space Shuttles used to land—the closest I ever got to fly on a Space Shuttle); and figuring out a way to do a complete, thorough analysis of a top secret experimental nuclear test facility without the benefit of a top secret security clearance. It was interesting, rewarding, and important work, but it was a level of abstraction away from actually touching—and knowing—the world.

My life took on another level of abstraction or two when I left that job and went to work for a software company, helping to communicate the value of the tools people use to manage and conserve the environment. I rationalized this move up the ladder of abstraction by asking myself—and answering—the following question:

> Is it better to have 100% hand in managing and conserving the environment at an incredibly small and local scale, or a 1% hand in managing and conserving the environment at a massive, possibly global scale?

It's a philosophical question. One is not necessarily better than the other. We need both local action and global action, and everything in between. I opted to give the 1% hand in global problem solving a try.

As my career advanced over the ensuing 20 years, I climbed both the corporate ladder, and the ladder of abstraction. I became a bit player in helping people understand and solve problems on the global stage, which is certainly something to be proud of. But over time, I almost completely lost touch with the landscape I had been so intimately involved with during my thesis research in the Mojave Desert, and even before that, as a teenager down in Africa. I was no longer touching the earth, but was looking at it from a distance.

How had everything gone so wrong? I was making a comfortable living and providing for my family, but had completely lost touch with the down and dirty details of the natural world I was trying so hard to understand and protect.

-----

It all became so clear. I really wanted to go back to Africa. Not to wander the halls of my old school, to see how much the houses and neighborhoods where I used to live in Quellerina and Morningside had changed, to try to reconnect with long-lost friends like Mark and Hayden, or to make yet another trip to my old hangouts like Kruger National Park, Blyde River Canyon, or Sterkfontein Caves. No, going to places old and familiar wasn't what I wanted. In fact, I didn't really want anything at all; I actually needed something.

I needed a vacation. But not a typical vacation. I longed for something more substantial, something more tangible; something that would let me get a real feel for the landscape, and maybe even contribute something, no matter how small, to society. I needed to once again get out and touch the blood red dirt, the prickly acacia, and the tall brown grasses; I wanted to

17

once again see with my own eyes the puffy white thunder clouds pasted against the cobalt blue sky; I craved the textures, the smells, and the tastes of Africa, that entire myriad of little things that individually seem almost trivial, yet taken together as a whole create a complete experience.

It was time to return to an experience that was as direct as possible. After much soul searching and research, I settled on a place that was completely new to me, yet seemed uncannily familiar: the Tuli Wilderness of Botswana. It was here that I hoped to cut through all the layers of abstraction and bullshit that had built up over the years. It was time to unclog my mental arteries. It was time to go back to the bundu.

I had been to a number of different places in Africa, but I had never before been to Botswana. The exact location, the name of the place on the map, and even exactly what I would be doing there seemed to mean very little. What was important was just going back, to simply experience whatever was there to experience.

"All I wanted to do now was get back to Africa."

— Ernest Hemmingway


-----


The salmon makes its epoch journey upstream to its primal home, to find a mate and die. But unlike the salmon, with my loving wife at home 10,000 miles away, I had no intention of mating while in Botswana, and was even less intent on dying there.

I had no expectations, other than to live life.

"Like a salmon, I can't forget the place I was born."

— Akira Kurosawa

# But First, a Brief Detour

I was dying to get to Botswana, to help out with the conservation research work being done in the Tuli Wilderness, and even more so to just immerse myself once again in the African landscape and lifestyle. But first I had to go through South Africa, my old home, to get there.

On the way to Botswana, I had to make an overnight stop in the town of Polokwane, South Africa to wait for my ride. I decided to add an extra day or two there, to see a little bit of a part of South Africa that I had never seen before—and to experience an Africa completely different than the Africa I would be getting in the Tuli Wilderness.

There were only three flights a day from Johannesburg to Polokwane, the first arriving at about 11 a.m. and the last arriving at about 5 p.m. Since my ride up to Botswana was picking me up at the airport at 6 a.m. on Wednesday morning, this meant I had to arrive in Polokwane on Tuesday and spend one night there.

After thinking about it, I decided to arrive in Polokwane on Monday afternoon, and spend two nights there before departing for Botswana. This would give me time to rest, relax, acclimatize, and adjust to the time change.

Rest. Relax. Adjust. It was a great idea. Then I started looking at a map.

Only a few miles away from my hotel was the Polokwane Game Reserve. Sandwiched between almost every kind of development imaginable, it was a wild island in the midst of modern chaos, like a jewel of nature carved out of the suburban jungle.

I made reservations to take a guided safari tour there on Tuesday. Polokwane Game Reserve versus the Tuli Wilderness would be the ultimate contrast, and my return to Africa would be a tale of two game reserves: one fenced, one free; one managed, one wild; one mostly modern, one almost primeval; Polokwane versus Tuli.

Walking across the tarmac and into the Polokwane Airport, I was instantly struck with how modern, clean, well designed, and just plain <u>nice</u> the facility was. I could have been standing in almost any small, ultra-modern airport in the world. Driving out of the airport towards my hotel, I was immediately reminded that I was in Africa. There were numerous haphazard wooden shacks set up on the side of the road—some even in the center divider—selling food. Surrounded by stacks of firewood, many were cooking potjie, a South African stew, in cast iron pots over open fires, the thick smoke rising from the fires. They were selling cheap, ready-made meals to the working poor. This was the Polokwane fast food district.

A lot had changed in my 35 year absence from southern Africa, but there was much more that was immediately familiar.

I was back.

-----

Situated on the Great North Road to Zimbabwe, Polokwane is in the heart of South Africa's Limpopo Province. Formerly known as Pietersburg, the town was renamed Polokwane after the fall of apartheid, when many geographic names with a colonial history were changed.

Today, Polokwane is the capital of the Limpopo province and boasts a bustling population of more than half a million people. When South Africa hosted the 2010 FIFA World Cup, it literally put Polokwane on the map: Peter Mokaba Stadium was built in Polokwane to host part of the tournament, one of five new stadiums built across the country to support the World Cup.

Before the Peter Mokaba Stadium came to town, the primary attraction in Polokwane was the Polokwane Game Reserve. Owned and operated by the provincial governing authority of the Limpopo province, it is one of the largest municipal game reserves in South Africa. Featuring a beautiful mix of grassland, acacia woodland, rocky outcrops, and open savannah, it is a completely fenced, carefully managed game sanctuary. It preserves one of the only remaining examples of the Pietersburg Plateau false grassland, a localized ecotone that is home to a number of rare birds and plants. The carefully selected combination of animal species in the reserve were free to roam anywhere they wanted on its 13 square miles of territory, but no further.

Compared to the Tuli Wilderness, the Polokwane Game Reserve is not a wild place; with no predators present on the property, it is a heavily managed, almost manufactured big game experience. But that's not to say it has no value. It plays a vital role in conservation, preservation, and education.

For me, the Polokwane Game Reserve was the polar opposite of what I would be walking in to in the Tuli Wilderness less than 24 hours later. But for many people living in modern Africa, it was as close as they were going to get to real, wild Africa; Polokwane Game Reserve was the New Wild.

-----

Lisa, my guide for the day in the Polokwane Game Reserve, picked me up at my hotel a little after 8 a.m. We drove in her pickup truck to a location just outside of the reserve where we switched into her Land Rover. I was the only one on the tour with her that day. "I normally don't do tours for less than six people," she said. "But you booked so far in advance, I decided to go ahead and take you." And just like that, for less than the price of a tank of gas back home, my simple little group safari had become a totally private tour.

The drive through the streets of Polokwane brought back so many memories of my youth...there's just something about driving around South Africa; it has a unique feel to it that's just impossible to describe. Or maybe it's just unique to me because I lived there at a formative time of my life.

We drove by the massive new Peter Mokaba Stadium. It was stunning, but it seemed like such a waste—similar to the Olympics, where a country spends a lot of money they can't really afford on massive sporting infrastructure improvements to impress the world, then when the event is over most of the new infrastructure falls into disuse and becomes a blight on the community. I wondered if this massive new stadium, plopped down seemingly in the middle of nowhere, ever got used now that the World Cup had come and gone.

Upon entering Polokwane Game Reserve, the first wildlife we saw was an ostrich. Soon after, it became quickly apparent to me that Lisa has a <u>lot</u> going on.  In addition to guiding safaris in her Land Rover, she has 23 horses and takes people on horseback riding safaris and tours; she also stables horses for other people; she has at least one rental unit in town; she runs a custom clothing business; she helps her husband with his environmental consulting business; and who knows what else.  She was a true entrepreneur.

I was amazed at how Lisa was able to drive her Land Rover down rutted dirt roads with one hand on the steering wheel and the other hand on her Blackberry, scanning the bush for wildlife while talking, texting, checking her emails, or surfing the web on her smart phone.  She's what I would call a hustler, but in no derogatory sense of the word; she was scratching out an existence here and there, doing this and that, all to make ends meet.  And rich or poor, white or black, urban or rural, I increasingly got the sense that this was the way that most people here survived; that in modern Africa, most everyone was a hustler.  At least the successful ones were.

Partway through our mini safari, Lisa stopped the vehicle in front of a large, beautiful tree with two huge male kudu standing underneath it.  But the kudu were just a coincidence—it was the tree she had stopped to tell me about.  It was a marula tree, which produces a fruit little-known outside of South Africa that is used to make a wonderful, creamy liquor called Amarula.  The seeds of the fruit are also ground up and release an oil that is used for beauty products.  But I actually heard very little of what she was saying, as I was completely overcome by an amazing fragrant smell wafting through my nostrils.

"That smell," I interrupted her, "...is that the marula tree?"

"No," she said, "I think what you're smelling is *Salvia africana-caerulea.*"

She jumped out and broke a small branch off of a nearby bush and handed it to me.

"Is that what you smelled?"

Yes, it was. It was South African sage. It was unlike the coastal sage, mountain sage, Mexican sage, and other sages I was so used to in California. This had a completely different smell to it. It took me a few minutes to realize, but I completely recognized the smell and it began to trigger memories of my adolescence in South Africa. It was something I had experienced in my wanderings through the bush in the vacant lots and other open spaces near where we used to live. It's amazing how something as innocuous as a small sprig of leaves and flowers from a bush can almost instantly transport the mind back in time some 35 years...

-----

Lisa was a big proponent of what I like to call "managed ecosystems," the Polokwane Game Reserve being a perfect example. Because the animals are protected (from humans, as well as from natural predators—there were no carnivores in the reserve), from time to time it becomes necessary to cull the herds in order to keep the population of animals at a sustainable level. In the Polokwane Game Reserve, instead of (directly) killing animals, their preferred method of management involves capturing surplus animals and legally selling them at auction. The animals are then purchased for relocation to private farms or game reserves, some of which may allow hunting, as well as for public game reserves and parks, zoos, etc.

I told Lisa about my upcoming trip to Botswana, and she was very familiar with the Tuli Block and the Northern Tuli Game Reserve. Five or six years prior, she had worked in the eastern section of the Tuli block, where the Shashe and Limpopo Rivers converge and where the borders of Zimbabwe, Botswana, and South Africa meet. She also leads safaris up there from time to time, and had just returned from one about three weeks earlier. She spoke of the extensive damage there from the recent floods, the most devastating of which may have been the removal of the topsoil from the landscape, as well as the destruction of much of the mature tree canopy along the Limpopo River corridor.

She went on at length about the elephant "problem" in the Tuli, and said that going back now, even after just five or six years, the change was dramatic—the Tuli area had become much more desolate looking, almost like a desert in spots, because of the elephants destroying the mopane trees. I asked her what had caused the dramatic increase in the elephant population in recent years—was it due to the lack of predation caused by the elimination of many of the predators in the area? She replied that carnivores really don't predate on elephants, except maybe on the very young or the very weak; no, the elephant population was not actually increasing, it was just that increased development throughout southern Africa meant that there was less natural area for them to forage for food. Their historic range has been heavily compromised by the encroachment of man. To make matters worse, in a move to establish a large trans-boundary park/reserve system, fences have been removed, which brings more elephants from the outside into the area.

Lisa is what I like to call a "true" environmentalist; like me, she believes that sometimes unpopular solutions are the best answer to vexing environmental problems. For example, sometimes you need to kill wild animals to help preserve a wild ecosystem live. She talked about how many so-called environmentalists want to protect and save animals at any cost, no matter how impractical, or how in the long term it very well could result in destroying an entire ecosystem.

In addition to the direct ecosystem benefits of culling, we also talked about more benefits to the local community. If carefully managed and controlled hunting is allowed in the form of culling, it can actually be an economic boon to the local community. The skin of the animal can be used to make clothing and shelter and for a variety of other purposes; the meat can be used to feed poor people; and in the case of elephants, you could even sell the ivory (if it wasn't illegal) and pour all of that money back in to the local community. Lisa's views were certain to be unpopular with the majority of people who refer to themselves as "environmentalists."

-----

Because of its proximity to such a large urban population, I asked Lisa if poaching was a problem in the Polokwane Game Reserve. She told me a story about how a few months earlier she had been leading a safari through the reserve on horseback when they came across a female rhinoceros with a tranquilizer dart stuck in her hind quarters. The dart had not fully penetrated the skin, so the tranquilizer had not taken effect. Lisa immediately used her cell phone to call the local authorities, who immediately sent out helicopters to search for the poachers. They never found the poachers, but a week or two later they found the carcass of a male rhino in the reserve that had been poached for its horn.

Before that incident, the rhinoceros population in the Polokwane Game Reserve had been 15; it was now down to 14. And, she told me, the day before our safari, in a different reserve about 30 miles west of Polokwane, authorities had found two more poached rhinos. The killing of rhinos for their horns has always been a problem in southern Africa, but in the last year or two it had escalated and was now reaching a level which was unimaginable.

She said that arresting one poacher is not the answer to the poaching problem; as soon as you arrest one, there are 5,000 more waiting in line to take his place. She sees the mafia as the real problem, and the solution is taking down the organized crime kingpins, not the individual poachers.

I disagree. I think the real problem is poverty, which is why people kill rhinos for their horns. As Jane Goodall says in her TACARE program, "to take care of the animals, you must first take care of the people." If the people are not taken care of, they are going to use any method possible to take care of themselves—even if that means poaching an endangered animal

After giving me some rough estimates of what various species of game animals would sell for at a legal auction, Lisa noted that the value of a rhino is next to nothing because they are such a huge liability to own. She sees legalizing the sale of rhinoceros horns to be a solution—taking them off of the black market and instead regulating the legal sale of the horns so that there is a financial incentive for ranchers to buy and breed rhinos, and to harvest their horns without killing the animals.

In general I agree with this idea, but would take it even further than that: using genetic engineering techniques, we should work to isolate the DNA for rhinoceros horn, and then create a hybrid rhino/cow that can be raised for milk and when it is mature can be slaughtered for its meat and horn—and then watch how quickly the world market for rhino horn collapses. While we're at it, let's also isolate the DNA for elephant ivory as well, and then create a hybrid cow with rhino horns and elephant tusks. It's an idea that may seem radical to some, but it's an idea whose time has come.

While we were driving around the reserve, Lisa pointed out a strange tree that I had never seen nor heard of before. There are many species of aloe native to South Africa, the most familiar to inhabitants of the rest of the world being aloe vera, but the "tree aloe" (*aloe barberae*) grows to a height of 30 feet or more and looks like a palm tree, except that at the top where you would expect to see palm fronds, there is an aloe plant. The aloe trees of Polokwane Game Reserve are all mature, nearing the end of their natural life cycle, and no young ones are sprouting to take their place. Lisa's theory is that the seeds were transported to the area and planted by the local inhabitants about 300 to 400 years ago, because you only find these plants in areas where there is also evidence of pre-colonial habitation.

-----

Polokwane Game Reserve is completely boxed in by human land uses. It's surrounded by a silica mine, a platinum smelting plant, coal mining, rock quarrying, residential housing, and agricultural and other land uses. And as South Africa increasingly becomes a player in the global economy, these types of activities are increasing at an alarming rate, with little or no government planning, regulation, or oversight.

30

Near the end of our suburban safari, Lisa stopped the Land Rover and said we would finish by taking a hike up a nearby kopjie (an Afrikaans term for a hill covered with rocks). We walked through the remnants of stone walls and a large hut circle constructed by the Bushmen who lived here 300 to 400 years ago, and she said that little is known about these archaeological sites because no research or study of them has been done.

We walked along the trail towards the top of the hill, looking for animals, when I smelled smoke and saw movement out of the corner of my eye in the bush off to the right. It was a person, who looked like he was barbecuing and having a picnic. As we approached, I realized that this was in fact our lunch! Even though I was the only one on her safari that day, Lisa had still gone through the trouble of having her assistant come out hours earlier to start a fire and cook us a meal.

She introduced me to her assistant, Joffrey, who had prepared a delicious meal of brown rice, Malay chicken curry, carrots, green beans, and butternut squash over the open fire. We also ate a salad made from fresh vegetables Lisa had grown in her garden, some fresh bread, and cheese. We sat down to an elegant lunch in the bush, the midday heat cut to a manageable level by the large shade trees we sat under. Dessert was a delicious lemon tart that Lisa had made from scratch.

Over lunch I got to know Joffrey a little better. Joffrey was nearing the end of a 3-month internship working for Lisa, sponsored by the local college where he was studying tourism. After working with Lisa, he was now interested in continuing with his studies and focusing on conservation biology. He was a very nice, smart young man, and an excellent chef. I believe he has a great future in tourism, wildlife management, or whatever he ultimately chooses. He represents much of the future of Africa.

On our short trek back to the Land Rover, Lisa pointed out an aardvark den in the middle of the trail, but the aardvark was nowhere to be seen as they are usually only active at night. Back at the vehicle, Lisa had me jump up into the tracking seat on the Land Rover and had me pose for a photograph. I felt a little uncomfortable doing this, as the next day I was to journey off to the Tuli Wilderness where I was to learn how to track African wildlife and, if I tried hard and got good enough at it and was able to pass my basic tracking test, I would earn the right to sit in the coveted tracking seat and lead a game drive.

As the day progressed, it got increasingly hot under the harsh African sun. The only thing that made it bearable was an occasional breeze, and the canvas canopy over the top of Lisa's open Land Rover. Most of the animals were hiding in the shade themselves now, so by the end of our safari we were seeing almost nothing.

On the drive back to my hotel, I noticed a huge crowd filling Peter Mokaba Stadium. I don't know exactly what they were there for, but it was good to see the place packed almost three years after the end of the World Cup, in the middle of the week. Ironically, at the nearby Polokwane Game Reserve, weekends can get quite busy, but weekdays can be practically empty. Lisa and I were the only two people I saw that Tuesday in the reserve. South Africans love their animals, but apparently they love their sport even more.

In the end, although we never saw any of the 14 elusive white rhino that day, we saw quite an impressive array of wildlife in the reserve, including ostrich, waterbuck, impala, duiker, kudu, zebra, blesbok, sable antelope, red hartebeest, tsessebe, blue wildebeest, giraffe, springbok, vervet monkey, a leopard tortoise, and countless birds.  Even more important than the animals I saw that day was the experience of the place—a carefully managed yet still intriguing game park, the polar opposite of what I was about to see in the Tuli Wilderness, and the company of a fine guide who made it personal.

-----

It was an exhausting day and I needed to get some sleep. The first of several rides would be waiting for me at 5:30 a.m. the next morning.  I checked, checked again, and verified everything a third time, but was still nervous, and if just one thing didn't go exactly as planned I might be waiting a week for the next ride. And as it turned out, I had reason to be nervous.

This was Africa, where everyone had a plan.

And this was Africa, where every plan always seemed to change…

# "-ish"

When we first moved to South Africa in 1976, the townhouse we rented in Quellerina didn't come with a phone. But that would certainly be easy enough to fix: we'd just drive down to the phone company, tell them we wanted one, and in no time at all we'd be chatting on the telephone with all of our friends. Right?

That's not the way it worked, at least not in South Africa in 1976. The typical wait for a phone to be installed was 6 to 12 months, so the phone company put us on a waiting list. Coming from the United States, we found this situation unbelievably primitive. If you wanted a phone in America, you would usually have it within 24 hours. But things were different in South Africa, apparently.

After waiting several months, we finally got our phone installed. And that was one of our many experiences with what we would come to learn was known as "African Time".

-----

When I returned to southern Africa in 2013, it didn't take long for me to once again start experiencing this indifferent attitude towards time. There's really nothing wrong with "African Time." That is, unless your schedule depends heavily on certain things happening at specific times. Like mine did.

"The single biggest problem in Africa is transportation," my van driver in Polokwane told me. "It sucks. Public transportation is

35

almost non-existent. We have very few buses and trains. So to move around, you either need to have a car, hire a driver, or fly. And it's expensive. Getting from point A to point B in southern Africa can be very difficult, and very expensive."

He was taking me from my hotel in Polokwane to the airport, where the second of three vehicles in my arduous overland trek to the Tuli Wilderness was to meet me at 6 a.m. But even that first of three stages almost didn't happen. After numerous emails to the hotel confirming and reconfirming my reservation for the airport shuttle, the night before I was scheduled to leave I had three different in-person conversations with the same people who had no idea what I was talking about and couldn't help me before I finally got a sense that things might actually work out.

It was almost like the entire journey was predestined to fail. The weakest link in my 10,000 mile journey from the suburbs of southern California to the wilderness of eastern Botswana seemed to not be connecting airline flights, but ground transportation. The real weakest link was that a vehicle left every Wednesday morning at 6 a.m. from the Polokwane Airport in South Africa to take volunteers like me up to the Tuli Wilderness in Botswana, and that if I missed that vehicle, I was totally screwed. My imagination started to create all kinds of bizarre scenarios where I missed my ride and ended up trying to hitchhike up to the Botswana border and pass through immigration without my sponsor present to grease the skids; or even worse, I was forced to just sit in my crappy hotel in Polokwane for a week, waiting for the next ride, and missing a week of working on the conservation program in the bundu.

I slept little on my last night in Polokwane. But when I was ready to go the next morning, the van and the driver were there on time, ready to take me to the airport. I even got to the airport about 15 minutes early. So much for "Africa Time"!

Knowing that it might be a long time before I had easy access to junk food again, I spent a long time perusing the vending machines inside the airport and filling up my luggage with unfamiliar brands of candy bars and suspect cans of lemonade. At about 6:20 a.m., just as I was starting to get nervous that my ride to the border may not show up, a lone car pulled into the parking lot.

I only talk out loud to myself when I'm very nervous or very relieved. "That's got to be him," I said out loud as a man about my age got out of the car and walked towards the entrance to the airport.

"Are you Matt?" he asked from about 20 feet away as he walked towards me.

"Yes," I said, extending my hand outward to shake his.

"What the hell are you doing here?" he asked. "I was at your hotel at 6 a.m. to pick you up, and the van driver told me he had just dropped you off at the airport!"

"They told me to meet you here…"

Since I was the only volunteer making the drive up to the Tuli Wilderness that week, it sure would have made a lot of sense for the driver to pick me up at my hotel instead of the airport, which was quite a distance out of the way for both of us. But my instructions from the volunteer coordinator were very clear: be at the <u>airport</u> by no later than 6 a.m.

A week later, when a new batch of volunteers arrived at the Tuli Wilderness, I noticed that one of them was carrying a water bottle from the same hotel I had stayed at in Polokwane. Later, I asked Bruce, who had reserved a spot in the program through the same group and stayed at the same hotel in Polokwane as me, if there was as much confusion with his transportation arrangements as there had been with mine.

"Not at all," he said. "They picked me up at my hotel exactly at 6 a.m., just like they said they would."

Well, OK then.

-----

An extended stay in primitive conditions in the Tuli Wilderness sounded like an incredible adventure, but from what I had read, just getting there was a big part of the adventure. I would be spending most of my time at Mohave Camp, a primitive camp without power deep in the Tuli Wilderness, with a chance to possibly stay two or three nights at Serolo Camp, a "luxury tented camp" much closer to the border with South Africa. But the single most exciting part of that adventure sounded like it might just be the Pont Drift border crossing from South Africa into Botswana.

When water levels were low in the Limpopo River, it was possible to drive across the sandy bottom at Pont Drift in a four-wheel drive vehicle. But in times of high water, such as the end of the rainy season when I was visiting, crossing the river by vehicle was impossible. Instead, you had to leave your vehicle on one side of the border and take a white-knuckle ride in a small cable car suspended over the river to the opposite bank, where another vehicle would hopefully be waiting to pick you up. The ride probably only lasted a minute or two, and if I was lucky, I might see a crocodile or two in the Limpopo below; if I was incredibly luck, I might possibly even see a hippopotamus. It wasn't that big of a deal, really, but I was excited about it. In my overactive imagination, there was something about it that encapsulated the feeling of the entire trip in to one brief experience. As silly as it sounds, I was looking forward to crossing the Limpopo in that flimsy little cable car more than any other single thing I had heard about on the entire trip.

And then the rains came. After a prolonged period of drought— an entire rainy season with virtually no rain—it finally rained in the Limpopo Valley. And it rained some more. And then it rained even more. Over a period of just three days, the area received almost a years' worth of rainfall.

And then the floods came. The Limpopo and other nearby rivers quickly overflowed their banks. Giant riverine trees that had grown along the river for decades or centuries were washed away in mere moments. Roads were damaged or destroyed. The cable car at Pont Drift I had so looked forward to riding in was made inoperable. Numerous camps in the area, including Mohave Camp where I was supposed to be staying, were damaged or destroyed. Looking at the map, I noticed that Serolo Camp was much closer to the Limpopo River than Mohave Camp was. If Mohave was heavily damaged, then certainly Serolo must have been completely destroyed.

I tried to get information about what was happening down there along the Limpopo, but as you can imagine it was rather difficult in that first week or so after the floods. Information was sparse. My mind began to wander, and I imagined the worst case scenario: my trip would be cancelled, or at the very least "postponed." So I started thinking about alternate adventures.

I looked in to going down to Australia or New Zealand to hike some of the famous trails and climb some of the famous mountains there. I thought about packing my car with my camping gear, mountain bike, kayak, rock climbing gear, snowshoes, and any other gear that would fit, and driving around the United States and Canada for three weeks to just experience...whatever. I considered trimming my vacation down to a week and hiking and camping in Death Valley National Park, just a few hours' drive from my house. After much thought, the option that looked most attractive was to cash out the two travel insurance policies I had taken out for my trip to Botswana and use the settlement money to buy a last-minute ticket to Ireland, where I would backpack across the country for three weeks by myself.

In the end, alternate plans proved to be unnecessary. I was informed that my adventure was still on, although the details were very vague. In a series of short and cryptic emails I was informed that the cable car had been damaged by the floods and that I would instead be crossing the river at Pont Drift in a small boat, and that a temporary tented camp had been established near Mohave Camp where the Botswana Conservation and Research Project volunteers would be staying until Mohave was reconstructed.

"Temporary tented camp." I imagined something even more primitive than Mohave Camp. Boy, was I in for a shock.

-----

On the drive to Pont Drift, I was informed that the cable car across the Limpopo was still not operational and that the water level was too high for crossing by boat. We were instead diverted to the west to a place called Platjan, where we could cross over the river via a concrete causeway into Botswana.

In another life—a life I had left temporarily in a little imaginary box at the last major city I had been in, sealed tightly and to be retrieved and opened only after my adventure in the bundu was over—I would have been seriously upset about the constant change that was happening with my trip plans. But oddly enough, that didn't happen. I didn't get upset. In a near delirious state from jet lag and exhaustion, at some point I stopped caring that the fine details of my itinerary were a moving target. "It will be what it will be," I thought. Good, bad, or ugly, I would be home in less than three weeks. And that's when I decided to let go, and to just take everything as it came. That's the moment that I truly arrived in Africa.

Once safely across the border and into Botswana, I asked Anneline, who was driving me on the third and final leg of my journey by ground, about the accommodations, and if Mohave Camp was operational yet. "We moved the program to temporary tented accommodations nearby," she said. "Before you leave, we should be able to move the program back to Mohave." And that was about it.

Too jet lagged to be any more curious, I drifted in and out of consciousness for the rest of the drive, imagining a dry, dusty, hardscrabble camp environment that made my visions of

Mohave Camp seem like heaven. So it came as quite a surprise when Anneline stopped the vehicle and said, "We're here."

I looked through the windshield of the Land Rover to see a large sign with white letters on a dark brown background greeting me that said:

"Serolo Camp."

Serolo had not been destroyed in the floods! I would be staying at a camp featuring luxury tents! That meant running water! A sink! A toilet! A shower! And electricity! With a large fan to cut the horrendous heat!

For a brief moment I was a little disappointed that I wouldn't be "roughing it" as originally planned. But I quickly realized how much more comfortable Serolo Camp would be. A once-in-a-generation natural disaster had resulted in a huge improvement in the quality of my accommodations. Despite the change, I would still be doing the exact same work for the Botswana Conservation and Research Program—and for the first week, I would have the camp all to myself. What luck!

I had earlier been informed that for the first week of the program, I was the only volunteer who would be present. But as I was to learn, everything changes. "We're a little full right now," Anneline said. "We have a large group of university students here, so we had to set up a small tent for you. But you'll only be there for the first two nights. They all leave on Friday morning, and then we'll put you in one of the tent cabins."

It seems that in Africa, everyone has a plan; and that plan always changes…

-----

It was in Serolo Camp that I first met Andrew, who led the Botswana Conservation and Research Program, and his significant other, Ash, who did all of the cooking at the camp. I would spend many hours with them over the course of two weeks, getting to know them as well as they got to know me. We would share some very special moments together in the bush—up close and personal with truly wild animals, in remote areas of indescribable beauty, and sometimes just simply sitting quietly and watching the sun as it slowly clawed its way below the horizon.

We also shared a lot of moments that in my previous life I would have found quite vexing. Many of these revolved around the challenges of trying to keep vehicles running in the bundu, which at times would have tried the patience of the Dalai Lama himself.

-----

Sundays were our "day off" in the program, but one Sunday I volunteered to drive up to help recover a vehicle we had managed to get stranded the evening before about 10 miles from camp. Andrew thought that I was volunteering to work on my day off because I was looking for any and every opportunity to see more wildlife and get out into the bundu. And yes, he was certainly right about that. But the real reason was because I wanted to experience more of this thing that Africa seemed to offer most—the changing of plans. Rather than just get annoyed or frustrated with situations, I was actually learning to enjoy it when these things happened.

When we were just about ready to jump into the "rescue vehicle," Andrew noticed a problem: there was no spare tire. He dug through the backs of some other disabled vehicles and eventually found a spare tire that looked to be inflated and happened to have the same bolt pattern as our vehicle. Just then, Bethule informed us that this vehicle also had a leaky radiator, so we should probably fill up several large containers of water to take with us so that we could make frequent stops to top off the radiator fluid. Then Andrew noticed that one of the rear tires of our vehicle was almost flat, which started a whole chain of events as we tried to get the air compressor at the main office to work so we could fill the tire. In the end, what should have taken us less than a minute ended up taking more than an hour. And rather than get exasperated at this comedy of errors, as I would have in a similar situation back at home, I instead relished every second of it.

-----

One night after we finished cleaning up after dinner and were heading back to our tents, I realized that we had been so engrossed in eating and talking that we had neglected to go over our plans for the next morning. The next day would probably be a "normal" day, meaning that we had to be at the vehicle ready to go and already having had eaten breakfast by no later than 6 a.m. Which in "Africa Time" really meant about 6:30 to 6:45 a.m.

"So what time are we meeting in the morning?" I asked.

"6 o'clock," Andrew replied.

"Alright, then," I said. "See you at 6."

"Right, 6 … ish."

"-ish," I said.

"-ish," he replied.

And after that, "-ish" became our motto. It came to signify firm plans that were written in stone, albeit a softer stone; plans that, though perfectly solid, would, come tomorrow, most likely be completely thrown out the window.

This attitude is not about a lack of caring, a shunning of responsibility, or laziness. It's about developing a comfort level with the simple fact that most days, for most things, in most circumstances, time really doesn't matter in any significant way. And it's not even just about time; it's about everything. In a way, it's about embracing the unknown. And it's liberating.

In Africa, everyone has a plan; and that plan always changes.

Or as I overheard someone say while in Botswana, "There is no time in Africa..."

If you don't like it, go somewhere else.

If you can learn to embrace it, then congratulations. And welcome to Africa.

That's "-ish."

# The Rhythm of the Bundu

Early on the morning of what was probably my third or fourth day in the Tuli, the sun still hidden behind the rocky hills, a slight chill in the air, Andrew stopped our vehicle right in the middle of the Mohave Highway. There was really no need to pull over to the side of the road to park here; the chances of seeing another vehicle out here were practically nonexistent.

As we jumped out of the vehicle, Andrew told us that our goal that morning was to hike around in the jumble of rocks between Horrible Hill and The Marsh and try to find the elusive spotted hyena den. Andrew had come close to finding it a few days earlier with the UK university student group; they had found the mother and her three pups and had watched and followed them for a long time, but it got dark before they could track the family all the way back to the den.

"Follow me, single file," Andrew said as he grabbed his rifle. "No talking, and try to be as quiet as possible. And whatever you do, don't run, unless I tell you to."

"Is it OK if I leave my backpack here and just take my camera?" I asked.

"Yes," Andrew said, giving me a very strange look. "Nobody is going to take your stuff out here."

My backpack contained <u>everything</u>—my wallet, all of my credit cards, my driver's license, and about $450 in cash in a mix of US

Dollars and South African Rand. And, perhaps most important, my passport was also in there. The vehicle wasn't just unlocked—it had no roof and no doors, and was completely open and exposed to the elements. Back at home, leaving anything in your car—especially if it was unlocked, even more so if it had no roof and doors—was an invitation to have it stolen. But I wasn't back home; I was 10,000 miles away, in a completely different world. I had only been in this place for a few days, and I was still trying to get a feel for the rhythm of the bundu. The habits learned from a life in "civilization" die hard.

We set out to the place where Andrew was fairly certain the spotted hyena den was located, a spot about 200 yards below where we left the vehicle. As we worked our way down, carefully and quietly, we heard another vehicle rumbling down Mohave Highway, coming towards us from the south. Although we were only a hundred yards or so from where we had parked, it was almost impossible to see all the way back up to the road because of the combination of topography and thick bush.

Still concerned about my precious belongings being stolen and me being stranded in the wilds of Botswana with no passport or money, I looked back nervously and was able to catch a glimpse of something white moving through the bush. Only a select few vehicles were legally allowed to be out here in the Tuli Wilderness, and I knew of just one that was white—Johann's brand new, white Toyota Hi-Lux pickup truck. But one of the trucks from nearby Talana Farms was white as well, and Talana staff sometimes trespassed over onto the Tuli Wilderness property for nefarious purposes.

I could hear the vehicle slow down as it approached ours, but it didn't stop; it continued past and started the rough decent down

Horrible Hill. As the sound of the vehicle faded off into the bush, we continued our search for the elusive spotted hyena den.

After about 15 minutes of quiet searching and observation around the point where he thought the den was located, Andrew determined that the hyenas were no longer there. As we turned around and started to head back up the hill towards our vehicle, we heard another vehicle approaching, this time from the north, climbing noisily up Horrible Hill.

The area we were in this time was even thicker and more dense, so much so that no matter how much I moved around, it was impossible to catch even the slightest glint of paint or other identifying mark on the second vehicle. But I could tell by the sound that the vehicle had stopped, and it was idling next to ours.

With every minute that went by without the sound of the idling vehicle moving on, my apprehension grew. By now they had certainly found my backpack and had finished rifling through my belongings. Take the money, I thought; I don't really care about that. Just leave my passport. What good would it do you to steal my passport? Do you realize all the pain you will cause me if you steal my passport?

Eventually we heard the sounds of the vehicle starting to move again, and it drove off. By that time it had been idling for so long next to ours that I was resigned to the fact that my passport and everything else was gone forever. I had already moved on, and was making mental preparations for my trip to the Botswanan capital of Gaborone, wondering how long it would take there to get my passport and credit cards reissued.

Of course, when we got back to the vehicle, everything was just as we had left it. Nothing was missing.

As we started to drive away, Ash said "What's this?"

She picked up something from the dashboard. It was a little bouquet of purple and white Botswanan wildflowers, carefully plucked and lovingly tied together with a thin blade of grass.

-----

Later that day, back at Serolo Camp, Johann walked in with a bag of groceries he and Anneline had just picked up in Bobonong, the closest town, about an hour away on rough dirt roads.

"So, Matt," he asked, "Did you get the little present I left for you guys this morning?"

Yes, Johann. We got it.

And I get it now.

# Off the Grid

While backpacking up to the Palisades Glacier in the Sierra Nevada Mountains in the summer of 2011, I got to thinking about our relationship with technology. When John Muir explored those mountains nearly 150 years ago, he would set out on long treks carrying "only a tin cup, a handful of tea, a loaf of bread, and a copy of Emerson." And yet there I was—ironically, deep in what is now known as the John Muir Wilderness— weighted down with a 40 pound backpack full of the latest examples of technological innovation: digital still and video cameras, GPS unit, LED headlamp, high-efficiency gas stove, water purification system, waterproof clothing, modern computer-generated maps, freeze-dried food, etc.

What would Muir think of this modern paradox, of escaping to the wilds of nature armed to the teeth with the latest technology?

-----

It's been more than 20 years since I regularly wore a watch. For the first 10 years, it was because I found that I never really needed to look at one—there was a clock built in to the dashboard of my car; at home, clocks (and appliances with built-in clocks) were never more than 10 feet away; I had clocks in my garage and in my backyard; at work, there was a clock on my computer, and if I was away from my office at a meeting, there were clocks in most of the conference rooms—cheap ones I had purchased with my own money and placed there, not necessarily to tell time, but with the idea that any boring meetings I was attending might conclude in a more timely manner if people knew how much time was being wasted; if not, at least I could easily extricate myself from a painful meeting by glancing at the clock and announcing that I needed to be somewhere else. And it wasn't exactly a lie; I actually did need to be somewhere else; anywhere but in that damn time-wasting meeting...and preferably outside...somewhere remote, somewhere natural...somewhere like the John Muir Wilderness...or the Tuli Wilderness...

When cell phones came along about 10 years ago, I suddenly had a "watch" of sorts again. It wasn't a bulky piece of metal strapped to my wrist, but I became reliant on it.

I had opted not to take a cell phone with me on the trip because of the supposedly spotty reception in the Tuli Wilderness, and because I really wanted to get away from all of that. I soon realized that not having a cell phone with me while travelling would not only deny me of communications, but it would also deprive me of any way of accurately and consistently telling time. I had flights to catch, people to meet, places to go, and a 10-hour time difference to deal with on top of all that. So I did the unthinkable. I went out and bought a watch.

Ironically, my quest to go technology free, or at least as "technology light" as possible, was quickly backfiring. And it wasn't just with the watch.

I usually charge my camera batteries by hooking the cameras directly to my computer through a USB cable. But not taking a laptop with me, I would have to take three separate battery chargers with me. And since my chargers all worked on standard 110 volt US current, I needed a 220 volt power converter, as well as the appropriate adapter for South Africa and Botswana.

It just kept getting more complicated.

-----

One of the attractions of heading off to the wilds of the Tuli Wilderness for an extended time was to get "off the grid", so to speak—and what better place to do that than at Mohave Camp, a remote, technology-challenged outpost where you were not even allowed to shower in the open bathrooms after dark because the elephants would come right up and snap off the showerheads looking for water; a place where laptop and camera batteries had to be charged for just an hour or two every night by running a power inverter off of the battery in the Land Rover.

When Mohave Camp was taken out of commission by the floods and we instead rolled into Serolo Camp, my decadent half loved the idea of staying at a "luxury" camp for the duration of my visit and taking advantage of plush creature comforts such as electricity and hot showers. But my primitive half, the half that loves sleeping in the dirt and redefining what "personal hygiene" means, was more than a little upset that I was missing out on my chance to truly go off the grid. But that was OK. I could live with it.

-----

The technology dichotomy in modern, rural Africa was quite interesting. I imagined I was going to a place where the sun is the power grid, the local stream is the water line, and talking around the campfire is the equivalent of the cell phone or social networking. Boy, was I wrong.

Over the course of my stay there, I saw many things.

Although I opted not to take my cell phone with me to southern Africa, I saw at least as much reliance on cell phones while there as you would see on a typical college campus back in the US. Everyone had cell phones—and everyone used them. Constantly.

Travelling to and from Tuli, it was not uncommon to see South African women with two cell phones—one for talking, and the other so that they could text while talking. And I thought people in the US were addicted to technology...

When driving across the Tuli Wilderness at night, besides the light on the vehicle and the stars in the sky, there was only one other light visible: a red light several miles south of the Limpopo River, inside South Africa, that marked the closest cell phone tower. Except for a few spots, it was usually fairly easy to get a cell phone signal in the Tuli.

There were two-way radios in each of the vehicles at Tuli, and they were used frequently for both day-to-day and emergency communication, but sometimes cell phones were more reliable. If your vehicle broke down and you radioed for help and nobody answered, you then called that person's cell phone—because you knew that they always answered their cell phone.

One night there were eight of us sitting around the campfire at Serolo Camp, and I was deep in conversation with another person.  As our conversation slowed, I noticed we had been the only two talking and glanced over towards the others.  All six of them were sitting with their faces down in their cell phones, frantically texting.

I can only hope they were not texting each other.

-----

Let's face it, technology—and our reliance upon it—isn't necessarily a bad thing.  It's easy to see the rampant destruction of the natural earth and blame modern technology, but that same technology also has a number of positive aspects.

Even though there was no Internet connection in the Tuli Wilderness, there was a laptop.  And we used it daily.  The goal of the Botswana Conservation and Research Project, after all, was data collection; what we did, every day, was to drive around the Tuli Wilderness and log data manually onto paper forms held on clip boards.  But every evening the data we had collected on various animals throughout the day had to be entered into the computer so that it could be shared with researchers around the world and thus contribute to the advancement of conservation science.

Another good example of the positive side of technology was Andrew's creative use of his iPod.  He had it loaded with guidebooks detailing the bird, mammal, and even fish species found throughout southern Africa.  He would identify a bird from a distance, for example, and then bring up that species on his iPod, show us detailed drawings and photographs of the species, and even play us an audio file of the birds call.

Leveraging the latest technology took the idea of a printed guidebook to an entirely new level of utility and interactivity.

Good or bad, technology was everywhere in Africa. I had gone into this trip thinking I was going to be almost completely off the grid and technology-free for a few weeks.

Ha!

-----

One night in camp as we were enjoying a very quiet dinner of mincemeat, mashed potatoes, and a fresh salad by candlelight, I heard a familiar sound that at first I paid no attention to. It took a second or two before I realized that it was a sound I shouldn't be hearing out here in the remote wilds of Botswana. Then Laura pulled her ringing cell phone out of her pocket and answered it.

"Hello, mummy," she said to her mother back in the UK. "We're having tea just now, can you phone back at 9?"

Technology. Sometimes we are master, and sometimes, it seems, we are slave.

# Diamonds in the Rough

Botswana is an interesting case study in what a country can do right in Africa. When Botswana first gained independence from the British in 1966, it had a GDP per capita of just $70. A paltry 22 citizens out of a population of 2 million had graduated from college, and only about 100 were high school graduates. The physical infrastructure was practically non-existent: in the entire country, there was less than 10 miles of paved roadway.

Soon after independence, diamonds were discovered in Botswana. The country is now one of the world's largest producers of diamonds, but has for the most part avoided the "resource curse" — the trap often seen where countries more heavily reliant on mineral exports experience more slowly growing economies. This "curse" is actually a practical result of poor wealth management in the face of a windfall. A poor country that suddenly finds itself sitting on one of the world's largest diamond deposits is like a poor person struggling to pay their rent who suddenly wins $50 million in the lottery. While it sounds like an amazing stroke of luck, rarely do these situations work out as well as envisioned for the country — or for the lottery winner.

Botswana is one of those rare examples that bucks this trend. It's an amazing success story. Careful management of its mineral wealth has transformed the country from one of the 25 poorest in the world to a thriving upper-middle income economy over the course of just a few decades. By 2012, literacy had increased to near 80%, and GDP per capita had risen from $70 to an astounding $16,200. Today, Botswana is one of the fastest growing — and least corrupt — countries in Africa.

One of the ways that Botswana managed to avoid the "resource curse" was to become less dependent on the revenues from the mining sector. The country did this by pursuing a strategy of economic diversification. One of the keys to this strategy has been to leverage its rich wildlife resources and abundant natural beauty for tourism. In fact, tourism is now an important component of the economy, and its importance is growing every year.

-----

In his State of the Nation address on November 5th, 2012, Botswana's President, Lt. Gen. Ian Khama, doubled down on this strategy by declaring that by the end of 2013 Botswana would implement a complete ban on commercial hunting of wildlife on public lands:

> "Of additional concern is the rise in cross border and domestic poaching incidents and trafficking of live predators, which are the subject of our new and evolving National Anti-Poaching Strategy. At the same time we have reached the decision to stop the commercial hunting of wildlife in public areas from 2014 as the shooting of wild game purely for sport and trophies is no longer compatible with our commitment to preserve local fauna as a national treasure, which should be treated as such."

It's a bold move, but not unprecedented in Africa. In 1976, Kenya instituted a similar ban.

While most conservationists and ecotourism operators have applauded Botswana's move, it is not without controversy. Some argue that a complete ban on trophy hunting is a recipe for disaster in terms of poaching, and point to Kenya's ban as a case in point.  Prior to the ban in Kenya, hunting concessions were granted for specific areas, and operators were responsible for managing their territories and controlling poaching.  With the ban on trophy hunting in 1976, the protection offered by the operators evaporated, and some observers say that poaching increased drastically in Kenya thereafter.

In some areas of Botswana, such as the Tuli Wilderness in southeastern corner of the country, management of elephant populations has been so wildly successful that the animals are overrunning the area and beginning to damage the natural ecosystem.  Culling of wild animals is always a contentious proposition; it's a management technique that's often necessary when humans significantly alter an ecosystem and need to stage interventions to regain a semblance of naturalness.  Some point out that commercial hunting of animals which will be killed by culling anyway is a win-win—it achieves the desired goal of reducing wild populations to a sustainable level while still contributing to the economy.

Will President Khama's initiative have the desired result and "preserve local fauna as a national treasure"?  Will it damage the tourism industry as hunters choose vacations in other countries where hunting is still allowed?  Will it lead to an increase in poaching as was observed under similar circumstances in Kenya?  Only time will tell, but on a continent plagued by mismanagement, poverty, corruption, and resource problems, Botswana's transition away from big game hunting to purely photographic ecotourism is yet another courageous move by a country with a remarkable track record.

-----

In certain sparsely vegetated areas of the planet, where the soil consists of a mixture of fine-grained particles (such as sand and dirt) and larger particles (stones of various size), an interesting erosional process takes place where wind, rain, and even surface water gradually remove the finer particles, but those forces are not strong enough to move away the larger particles. The result is that a surface of tightly-packed, seemingly interlocking, almost cobblestone-like rocks of various shapes and sizes develops over time, forming what is called "desert pavement."

Once desert pavement becomes established, most erosion stops as there is no more fine grain material left exposed to the elements. It also becomes more difficult for vegetation to gain purchase in such a near-impenetrable environment. The stones take the erosive forces and the oppressive heat in stride, and eventually develop a darkened sheen on their exposed sides referred to as "desert varnish." It's a beautiful sight to see a landscape covered in desert pavement, and it can be nirvana for rock collectors.

In parts of the Tuli Wilderness, I could see similar processes taking place. In most areas, the assortment of stones on top of the soil fell far short of producing a continuous "pavement," but you could tell that over hundreds or thousands of years the soil had eroded and the concentration of stones was gradually increasing as the surface elevation dropped. Give it another few thousand years, and maybe some of these areas would be covered in their own version of desert pavement.

-----

In addition to diamonds, Botswana is also known for another type of beautiful, if much less valuable, gemstone: agates. The agates of Botswana are commonly used to produce inexpensive jewelry, and they come in a wide variety of colors and shades. The Tuli area is literally littered with agates in many places, strewn across the landscape like seeds sown across an open field. Quartz crystals are also very commonly found there.

The first time I found an agate on the ground in the Tuli Wilderness, I couldn't help but feel a little excited: could it possibly be a diamond? Of course, it wasn't; but it was a beautiful piece of rock, and I carefully tucked it inside my pocket. Before long, I had several pounds of agate and quartz in a bag back in my tent, each new find a little more beautiful than the previous. I had to stop this collecting or I was certain that the airline was going to charge me an excess baggage fee on the trip home. Unless I found diamonds. If I found diamonds, I was picking all of them up.

One day while we were walking around searching for wildlife, Ash picked up a lovely milky-white stone that was protruding from the ground where it had been positioned for dozens of years or more as the red dirt around it was gradually eroded by the wind and rain. I had seen the stone from a distance and had planned to pick it up myself because it looked particularly diamond-like, but she got to it first.

"I think this is a diamond," she said.

Andrew looked at it skeptically. "It's an agate."

"A what?"

"An agate."

"Are you sure it's not a diamond?" she asked.

He looked at it again. "Agate."

"I still think it's pretty" she said as she folded her fingers around it. She was going to keep this one.

A little while later, she said to Andrew, "There <u>are</u> diamonds here, right?"

"There are diamonds <u>everywhere</u> in Botswana," Andrew replied.

"So what would you do if you found a big diamond here?" Ash asked.

"Well, you wouldn't say you just found it," Andrew replied. "It's a family gemstone which has been passed down for many generations. That's how you got it. That's your story."

-----

A week later, towards the end of my stay in the Tuli Wilderness, we were hiking down from Eagle Rock and we came across an area that had seen a lot of erosion, leaving a particular high concentration of strikingly beautiful agates. Despite my earlier vow to not do so, I once again found myself rapidly filling up my pockets with these lovely gemstones. Excess baggage fees be damned.

Ash was also aware of the abundance of agates in this area, and she was scanning the ground in front of her.  As she stopped to pick up a particularly interesting milky-white agate, she looked back at me.

"I'm still looking for my diamond…"

# The Great Grey-Green, Greasy Limpopo

"What does the Crocodile have for dinner?" asks the Elephant's Child.

"Go to the banks of the great grey-green, greasy Limpopo River, all set about with fever-trees," the Kolokolo Bird replies, "and find out."

—from Rudyard Kipling's *How the Elephant got his Trunk*

-----

One of my most vivid memories from my childhood in South Africa was the morning I was strolling along the banks of the Sabie River by myself and came face to face with a crocodile.

In August 1977, on my second trip to Kruger National Park, we spent five days exploring, seeing sights both new and familiar, the kind of roaming where the journey itself is the destination, when the unexpected things along the way are what you actually came for, where "Point A" and "Point B" are necessary evils, and the jagged line drawn between them is the real reason you're there.

On our last morning at Skukuza Camp in Kruger National Park, I awoke before everyone else and left our hut to walk down to the Sabie River. In the pre-dawn light, there was a comforting stillness. A light mist danced playfully above the river, not unlike the light fog hovering hazily over my still half-asleep brain. The river was moving slowly but confidently towards me, its surface nearly as flat and smooth as a sheet of glass, yet still making that indescribable sound that only strong, slow moving rivers make.

I was 14 years old, in a remote, wild section of Africa, by myself, and it was practically dark outside. But it never occurred to me that walking down to the river that morning might not be the brightest idea I ever had.

I rubbed my sleepy eyes and scanned the area for any signs of wildlife. Even though we were in the relative safety of the camp, you could never be certain. But there was nothing. Not even the chirp of a bird, or the rustling of a baboon in the trees overhead. There was nothing but a profound stillness, a deep silence, punctuated ever so slightly by the nearly inaudible heartbeat of the river flowing confidently by.

Looking upstream, I noticed a very slight movement. Ah, but it was a just a stick floating slowly towards me, propelled gently by the tug of the mighty Sabie River.

My eyes fixated on the floating stick, simply because it was the only thing in the river that revealed any sense of movement. In fact, it was the only thing in the entire landscape moving at that moment, save for my body shifting slightly back and forth as I balanced myself on the riverbank.

I continued to watch the stick as it progressed ever closer. As it floated gradually downstream, it also moved ever so slightly from the middle of the river towards the bank where I stood. Before long, it was only about 30 feet away, and maybe 15 feet off the bank—close enough that I was starting to make out much more detail on it, including what appeared to be two leaves attached to the stick.

And then the leaves blinked.

-----

When the Limpopo River overflowed its banks in January 2013, a lot changed. Age-old trees were gone in an instant, and riverbanks were eroded and fell away, transforming the look and feel of the landscape. Debris was deposited high in the branches of those trees that survived the flood, and sometimes in that debris we even saw the carcasses of waterbuck and other animals that had not been able to escape the oncoming torrent quickly enough.

Another change that took place was in the crocodile population. The Limpopo, like other rivers in southern Africa, is natural habitat for *Crocodylus niloticus*, also known as the Nile or African crocodile. Like so many other species in Africa, its numbers have been gradually decreasing due to both direct and indirect conflicts with man. But a funny thing happened during the floods. The crocodile population in the Limpopo increased by orders of magnitude overnight, at a scale that would make the heads of most restoration biologists and conservationists spin.

Along the southern banks of the Limpopo River about 20 to 30 miles upstream from Serolo Camp lies Rakwena Crocodile Farm, a local tourist attraction which is also a working farm where crocodiles are raised for their skin and meat. As the storm surge approached, the owner of the farm was faced with a tough decision: do nothing, and watch the pens holding the crocodiles be destroyed by the raging flood waters; or open the gates to the pens and let the water rush through, which would cause much less damage to his structures, but would release all 15,000 of his crocodiles into the Limpopo.

The owner of the farm decided to open the gates. The result was that the Limpopo suddenly was repopulated with crocodiles, to levels not seen in a hundred or more years, maybe even back to pre-colonial levels. If ever there was a river that Indiana Jones could cross simply by running from croc to croc, it was the Limpopo after the floods of January 2013.

-----

Most days at Serolo Camp, we jumped into one of the four-wheel drive vehicles and drove many miles away to perform our daily game counts and other duties. But once or twice a week, we ditched the vehicle and walked, venturing just two to three miles away from camp. And most of these treks ended up down at the Limpopo River, that thick watery line dividing Botswana and South Africa that we could not cross due to the combination of border restrictions and large carnivorous reptiles.

The dominant feature of the Tuli landscape is the mopane tree. In most places, the mopane trees are clipped down to the height of a large shrub by the ever-present elephant herds. But as you approach the Limpopo River, about half a mile out, the landscape starts to change noticeably. The mopane trees gradually decrease in number, to be replaced by the fever trees that Kipling wrote about in *How the Elephant got his Trunk*. Unlike the name would imply, ingesting the leaves of the fever tree does not cause a fever, but instead causes diarrhea. So the elephants steer clear of eating them, and they grow tall along the wide banks of the Limpopo thanks to a combination of the abundance of water and lack of regular trimming.

When we got to the edge of the river, we dropped down a bank cut steep by the recent flood, jumped across a small, shallow channel of water, and then walked out onto a large sand bar that stretched for several hundred yards out into the Limpopo like a low island. Andrew was in the lead with his big rifle, watching warily for any crocodile surprises.

The sand was crisscrossed with crocodile tracks, many of them relatively small, but some large enough that you could fit your entire hand inside a single footprint and still have plenty of room to wiggle your fingers around. And it wasn't just the tracks that we saw; we also saw the crocs. Lots of them. It was hard to look anywhere and not see one. Or two. Or more. In one location, I saw three crocs so close together that I had to take a picture of them. When I got home and examined the photo more closely, I counted six crocs in the frame, and possibly a seventh.

Johannes had lived his entire life, more than 70 years, in this very spot. He had never seen this many crocodiles in the Limpopo before

Even though all of these crocs were technically the same species, they were not all wired the same. As you approached the river from a distance, you might be able to look out and count half a dozen crocs or more. As you walked closer, suddenly one or two of them would bolt into the water and be gone in a flash. The rest wouldn't even budge. As you walked closer, and closer still, you expected them to jump into the water at any moment, and braced yourself for the startling flash of green and splash of water they would make when it happened…except that it never happened. You might have to get just a few feet away and tap these crocs on the head with a pebble before you saw any type of reaction from them at all. That was the difference between the wild crocs of the Limpopo, and the ones that had spent all but the last month of their lives in the domesticated environment of Rakwena Farm.

While I was surprised that we were able to get so close to some of the crocs on the Limpopo River, my closest encounter with the crocodiles of Botswana came not on the Limpopo. It was on the Motloutse, a tributary to the Limpopo.

-----

About every other day, we drove up to the Motloutse River overlook on the eastern edge of the Tuli Wilderness. It was almost guaranteed that a trip there would result in an elephant sighting, and on a really good day we might see two or three herds there in less than an hour. On this day, however, there were no elephants. We sat on our rock about a hundred yards from the parked vehicle and waited for a while, passing the time by identifying the birds nesting in the tree above us as well as those picking for bits of food in the sand bars of the Motloutse, but the elephants never came. So we decided to hike further north up the west bank of the river, to see what we could find up there.

The only other footprints we saw on the rough trail we followed were those of an impala, a hyena or two, and a leopard. The trail disappeared as the rocky bank became more of a cliff for a hundred or so feet, but then it opened up again, and we were left standing on large flat rocks at the edge of the slow-moving

Motloutse.  Off in the distance, a black-backed jackal lazily searched for scraps of food along the opposite shore.  A few birds fluttered by, but they were nothing we had not already seen.  Off in the distance, a small crocodile quickly dove into the river—one of the timid ones.  Maybe the farm-raised crocs from the Limpopo had not yet managed to move this far up the tributary.

Andrew and I stood at the edge of the rocks, him holding his rifle, me holding my camera, scanning the river and the banks and the mopane trees beyond for any hints of wildlife.  Our toes dangled over the edge of the rocks just a foot or two above the river, which this late in the season still held some water but every day was drying up a little bit more.

"Hello!" Andrew said, looking directly below us through the shallow, almost stagnant pool at our feet.  "There's your croc, Matt!"

There, just a few feet from our toes, was a croc about four feet long, barely visible through the grey-green and greasy water.  The longer we stared at it, the clearer the image became, until we noticed there was a second croc lying right next to it.

So what does the crocodile have for dinner?  Luckily we never found out.

# My Feathered Friends

Birds are magnificent, fascinating creatures. The variety of colors, shapes, and sizes of these feathered beasts is like an artist's palette on steroids. Who has never watched a bird in flight and been envious of the freedom it represents?

I really never was much of a "birder"—the type of person who roams the country, or the world, chasing down the winged wild and the avian exotic, travelling to remote corners of the globe with the hope of catching even a brief, fleeting glimpse of a rare specimen—but my youth in southern Africa almost turned me in to one.

Almost…

-----

As a teenager I had gone to Africa in the 1970s with images from *National Geographic* magazine seared into my brain. The animals would be monstrously large, they would be dangerous, and they would be everywhere. In fact, to protect myself while walking to school or playing in the front yard with my new friends, I would probably have to carry around an elephant gun. And maybe a huge knife as well.

What I didn't expect was that in many ways, the reality of our living situation in South Africa was not too unlike where we had come from in southern California: we settled comfortably into a suburban housing tract. Oh, there certainly were big differences.

Acacia trees covered with large thorns waiting to shred clothes and skin. Cobras hidden in the brush ready to sink their fangs into anything that moved. Chameleons as big as your hand blending in to the trees or the bushes or whatever they happened to be in front of at the time. Termite mounds of blood-red dirt six feet tall stabbing the pure cobalt sky. No, roaming around this neighborhood wasn't exactly the same as where I had come from. At least there were no elephants running through our backyard, lions stalking me on the way to school, or zebra eating the flowers next to the driveway.

Without the threat of imminent attack from a herd of wild animals, just what exactly was an American teenager trapped in Africa with lots of free time on his hands supposed to do? Faced with the reality of my new suburban jungle, I abandoned my quest for big game and instead set out on a months-long adventure to chase those wild animals that make their habitat everywhere on this modern planet, no matter how urbanized: birds. I really wanted to see typical African "big game," and I did on those occasions when we traveled to nearby parks or nature preserves, but life goes on; even when you live in Africa, you can't be on safari every day. But the birds were everywhere, and I could watch them any day, anytime, anywhere.

-----

I quickly became familiar with all the different species of exotic birds around me. Of course, there were the sparrows and herons and other birds you can commonly see in other parts of the world, but in southern Africa I got to see a much wider range of avian creatures, with exotic names like African Fish Eagle, Red-Knobbed Coot, Lilac-breasted Roller, Southern Yellow-Billed Hornbill, Egyptian Goose, African Hoopoe, Acacia Pied Barbet, Crested Barbet, Fork-Tailed Drongo, Bokmakierie, Cape

Sparrow, Gray Go-Away Bird, Burchell's Coucal, Village Weaver, and Southern Masked Weaver.

The best part was that the majority of these beautiful creatures were present not just in national parks or game preserves, but also in the vacant fields in the neighborhood, and even in my own backyard. Bird watching was like a poor man's safari.

I wandered through the bush, "hunting" these feathered wild animals down with my "gun" — an old 35mm camera and a gigantic 500mm telephoto lens attached to a tripod. Stealing a large knife from the kitchen to use as my make-shift machete, I taught myself how to make bird blinds from dried grass and brush. I learned how to spot birds from great distances and stalk them until I was just a few yards away. I learned how to crudely call some of them. After a while, you might say that I even started to think like a bird. But despite the countless hours, the skills learned, and all of the beautiful birds seen, I never really did become a "birder".

-----

The Northern Tuli Game Reserve is one of the best places in southern Africa for birders, with more than 350 different species of birds having been spotted in the area. For my first trip back to the bundu after an absence of 35 years, I was much more interested in seeing mammals than I was birds, but this wasn't a sightseeing vacation or a guided safari; I was volunteering for a conservation project, and would gladly do whatever they wanted or needed me to do. It's just that I secretly hoped that whatever it was they decided to occupy my time with, none of it involved birds. As it turned out, birds were a big, important aspect of the project.

If the Botswana Conservation and Research Project in the Tuli Wilderness can be boiled down to a single defining element, it's simply this: data. New volunteers are presented with a stack of 20-odd forms on clipboards that need to be carried along on all outings. Learning which forms to use under which circumstances, and the correct nomenclature and abbreviations to use when filling them out, takes a little getting used to. But before long it became almost automatic; it was just something you did as you came across yet another animal or bird on the side of the dusty dirt road.

When we approached any wildlife that required data collection, the normal procedure was to stop the vehicle and immediately start observing. Each person in the vehicle has a specific assignment or two, and those assignments differed each day—you might be tasked with an overall count of the herd, or counting something more specific like adult males, females, or juveniles; or maybe that day you were responsible for interpreting the map and recording the location of the animals and their direction of movement.

One day while out driving we came across yet another herd of elephants. As Andrew slowed the vehicle to a stop, we were already reaching for our clipboards and binoculars, ready to spring in to action—except for one person, a new volunteer, not yet fully initiated into the program, who stood up excitedly, camera pressed closely to her face, and began rapidly firing off pictures of the elephants as if she was on some sort of leisurely safari.

"This is not a vacation," Andrew said sternly. "Your job here is to collect data. When data collection is done, if there's time, then you can take your photographs."

-----

Ironically, the only exception to this "data first, photographs later" rule was birds. And for good reason.

There are a lot of birds in the Tuli. And unless you're a hardcore, experienced birder, identifying and keeping track of all of them can be a nightmare. Just in the last week of February, in between tracking and collecting data on animals, doing road repairs, hunting for snares and other signs of poachers, entering data into the computer, washing dishes, and other miscellaneous work tasks, we were able to identify an astonishing 62 unique species of birds present in the Tuli Wilderness:

- Arrow-Marked Babbler
- Crested Barbet
- Southern Carmine Bee-Eater
- European Bee-Eater
- White-Fronted Bee-Eater
- Kori Bustard
- Diderick Cuckoo
- Great Spotted Cuckoo
- Red-Chested Cuckoo
- African Mourning Dove
- Cape Turtle Dove
- Laughing Dove
- Namaqua Dove
- White-Faced Whistling Duck
- African Hawk Eagle
- Black-Chested Snake Eagle
- Brown Snake Eagle

- Wahlberg's Eagle
- Western Cattle Egret
- Lanner Falcon
- Red-Billed Firefinch
- Egyptian Goose
- Helmeted Guineafowl
- Hamerkop
- White-Crested Helmetshrike
- Grey Heron
- Southern Red-Billed Hornbill
- Southern Yellow-Billed Hornbill
- Pied Kingfisher
- Woodland Kingfisher
- Red-Crested Korhaan
- Blacksmith Lapwing
- Crowned Lapwing
- White-Crowned Lapwing
- Monotonous Lark
- Fiery-Necked Nightjar
- Black-Headed Oriole
- Ostrich
- African Scops Owl
- Spotted Eagle Owl
- Verreaux's Eagle Owl
- Pearlspotted Owlet
- Redbilled Oxpecker
- Black Backed Puffback
- European Roller
- Lilac-Breasted Roller
- Grey-Headed Bushshrike
- Lesser Grey Shrike

- Southern Grey-Headed Sparrow
- Chestnut-Backed Sparrow-Lark
- White-Browed Sparrow-Weaver
- Natal Spurfowl
- Swainson's Spurfowl
- Meves's Starling
- Marabou Stork
- White Stork
- Barn Swallow
- Cape Vulture
- White-Backed Vulture
- Willow Warbler
- Bearded Woodpecker
- Cardinal Woodpecker

It's an impressive list for such a short period of time; an unusual, but not unprecedented, number of individual species to see in just a week. And in the first few days of March, we added another 10 bird species to our Tuli observation list:

- Little Bee-Eater
- Yellow-Crowned Bishop
- Fork-Tailed Drongo
- Knob-Billed (Comb) Duck
- African Hoopoe
- African Grey Hornbill
- Glossy Ibis
- African Sacred Ibis
- Wooly-Necked Stork
- Kurrichane Thrush

With so many birds, and the only expert birder amongst us being the program leader—whose intent was not to do our work for us, but to make us learn to do the work ourselves—it was hard, and at times extremely frustrating, trying to identify every species.

I soon realized that birding can be a hell of a lot of fun if you have someone with you to tell you everything you're seeing. At least it was that way for me. I'm sure "real" birders get a thrill of doing the identification themselves. But when we stopped to identify a bird you didn't already know, Andrew would throw the book at you—the bird book, that is—and tell you to look it up.

Not knowing much about birds, my preferred method of identifying a particular species was slightly less haphazard than random guessing; I would start on the first page of a tome describing 3,675 different bird species and thumb through a page at a time, hoping that with a little luck I might recognize the creature that was in front of me. It was a method that rarely if ever resulted in correctly identifying the species, and instead resulted in extreme frustration and disdain for the entire concept of birding.

My only hope was that the bird would fly away before I further embarrassed myself trying to guess the species, which was actually a fairly common occurrence. Since birds are by definition a flighty bunch, often before we could even approach the bird at a close enough distance to have a decent chance of identifying it, it had already flown away. After about the fifth time this happened, Andrew told us the exception to the "data first, photography later" rule.

"When we drive up to a species of bird you can't identify," he said, "someone with a good telephoto should immediately take a photograph of it. That way, if it flies off before you can identify it, you can look at the photo back at camp and identify it." Back in the safety and comfort of camp, with no pressure, I could take all the time I needed to shuffle through the guidebook and try to identify the birds we had seen that day.

What I learned from this project, as I was also simultaneously learning with the identification of animal tracks, was that the key to identification is starting at a higher level. Certain families of birds have distinguishing characteristics that you can memorize, and if you can't identify a particular species this can at least help you put the unknown bird into one or two broad categories. Then, through the process of elimination, you may only have to look at 5 or 10 or 15 birds in the guidebook, rather than all 3,675. This technique makes so much sense to me now; never having had any formal training from an expert birder until that point, all of my previous experiences had been about randomly opening pages in a book and hoping that I'd eventually stumble upon the proverbial needle in the haystack.

Now I knew the secret of the birders. There was an easier way. They weren't just people with photographic memories or insanely awesome memorization skills. There was a method to their madness. I suddenly saw birders in a completely different light.

-----

One day towards the end of my stay in the Tuli, as we were driving back to camp after a long, productive morning game drive, on a road we seldom travelled across the base of Kudu

Ridge, we all saw a familiar fluttering in the trees off to the right. Oh no, not another bird, I thought. Can't we just drive back to camp in peace? Andrew stopped the vehicle, and instantly my blood pressure started to rise and a bead of sweat formed on my forehead. I knew what was coming next...

"Does everyone see it?" he asked. A low, grumbling, barely audible "Yes..." emanated from several parts of the vehicle, not unlike a group of unhappy middle school students responding sarcastically to the teacher's question of "Isn't everyone excited about this test?"

"Matt," he continued, "what's the bird?" I automatically reached down to pick up the guidebook, then hesitated. "Wait," I said, "isn't that a ... uh ... a ... Namaqua Dove?"

"Yes!" he replied. "Very good, Matt."

Andrew was happy with my progress; the other volunteers, who were still relatively new to the program, were no doubt envious of my incredible birding skills; and I was a little bit proud of myself as well. Or at least I should have been proud of myself. Instead, my first reaction, screamed silently to myself, was GOOD LORD, GET ME OUT OF THIS GOD FORESAKEN HELLHOLE BEFORE I BECOME A DAMN BIRDER!

But as Andrew started the vehicle and we began moving again down Ridgeback Road, a funny thing happened. A little voice in my head started to whisper that maybe birding wasn't that bad after all; maybe it was something I could start to enjoy.

Luckily, the rumbling of the engine and the incessant squeaking of the battered suspension quickly drowned out that insane little voice calling me towards the birding life.

-----

The voice in my head had been temporarily silenced, but the birds themselves kept calling me back. And one bird in particular called louder than all of the others.

From the moment I first set foot in Botswana, I heard the distinct call of the African Mourning Dove. It would become the soundtrack to my time in the Tuli—an incessant, non-stop sound that for me came to define the place more than any other single experience.

In one of the guidebooks to the birds of southern Africa that we used throughout the project, they referred to the call the African Mourning Dove makes as "the sound of Africa," and described the call itself as "*krrrrr-ooOO-oo.*" But the first time I heard this bird, I didn't hear "*krrrrr-ooOO-oo*"; I heard "*Bots-WAH-na.*" I heard it from the first minute of my first day to the last minute of my last day in the Tuli, and I heard it in my dreams every night. I heard it in my ears, and in my imagination, that bird saying "*Bots-WAH-na*" over and over and over again. It was at the same time something both very comforting to hear 24 hours a day, and something that could have easily driven me to the brink of insanity.

If ever there was a voice in my head telling me not to dismiss the birds as lesser creatures undeserving of study and admiration, it was the African Mourning Dove.

*Bots-WAH-na.*

*Bots-WAH-na.*

*Bots-WAH-na.*

It's a sound that still haunts me, and it's something I will remember every day for the rest of my life.

-----

One night sitting around the campfire at Serolo Camp in the Tuli Wilderness, we were telling stories about tourists—bad tourists—and all of the really bad tourist stories seemed to be about Americans. As the only American at the campfire that night, I was definitely the minority; but I made no attempt to justify the typical "Ugly American" attitude and behavior you typically see when Americans travel abroad. Instead, I wholeheartedly agreed with what they were saying; I had seen it too often myself, and decided the best defense of my fellow Americans was to set a better example myself, and show this mixture of South African, British, French, and Canadian nationals that the stereotype might be common but that it was not always true.

My favorite Ugly American story that night was that of the middle-aged American tourist sitting outside at one of the game camps in South Africa, taking in the magnificence of the unspoiled landscape, and then saying to his guide, "It's so beautiful here. Absolutely breathtaking. Tell me, who does your landscaping?"

After a while, my new multinational friends seemed to either run out or tire of telling tales about "Ugly Americans."

"You know who are the absolutely worst people to guide?" asked Andrew. "In my experience it's definitely the Japanese. The problem is that they come with lists, and they're even worse than the birders are with their lists. We'll see an animal they haven't seen before—say, a leopard—and I'll drive close to it and turn off the vehicle. They'll immediately pull out their checklists, mark off 'leopard', and say 'OK, let's go.' We're literally there less than ten seconds, and they've seen enough of the leopard—of all leopards. All they want to do is find another animal they haven't seen yet, check it off their list, and move on to the next animal as quickly as possible."

It seems that we humans can't ever really just completely relax and enjoy nature on its own terms. At least very few of us can. Instead, we latch on to our precious hobbies, such as hiking, hunting, skiing, photography, gold panning, or watching birds or tracking wildlife; we become so absorbed in our little rituals— like making lists and checking them off—that we obsess about them, focusing so much on the mechanics that we start to forget about the beauty and the joy of the act itself—the reason we were drawn to that particular activity in the first place. With pastimes that involve enjoyment of the outdoors, we often take them to such an extreme that we forget what we probably never really wanted to know to begin with: that we don't actually care much for the activities themselves; they are just excuses to get outside.

This scenario would play out many times in my own life, as I meandered through phases of fishing, mountain biking, rock climbing, running, backpacking, kayaking, mountaineering, and other outdoor activities. But looking back at my time spent chasing the birds through the bundu, it wasn't at all about the birds. It was just the first of many times in my life that I became absorbed in a ritual as an excuse to simply get outside and touch nature.

*Bots-WAH-na.*

*Bots-WAH-na.*

*Bots-WAH-na.*

# A Day in the Bundu

Out deep in the bundu one morning, we approached yet another dry river crossing. Andrew looked especially concerned with this one; apparently the bank closest to us had severely eroded in the floods the previous month, and the drop from the road high on the bank down into the sandy bottom was too steep for the vehicle to safely navigate. But he really wanted to get to the other side. There was another way to get to where he wanted to go, but that would require a detour of many miles.

Andrew, Ash, and I spent the next half hour moving dirt with a horribly inadequate short-handled shovel. Every time I thought we were done, the notoriously meticulous Andrew would say "we need a little bit more dirt over here..." Eventually we had reconfigured the steeply cut bank into one that sloped just enough where Andrew thought he could get down it without getting stuck or damaging anything.

"You two wait out here," he said as he locked the front hubs, put it into four-wheel drive mode, and got back in and started the engine. "I need the vehicle to be as light as possible."

He inched forward slowly, and dropped down the embankment without the slightest problem. Once into the soft sand of the riverbed, he accelerated quickly; there was another hill to climb on the other side, less steep, but more sandy, and he was concerned about getting stuck there so he needed all the momentum he could get.

He never made it that far. Two thirds of the way across the sandy river bottom, he slowed, and then stopped, the wheels still spinning violently, sand flying everywhere in a gigantic pink cloud. In a desperate attempt to not get stuck, he threw the vehicle into reverse, then forward, and then reverse again, then forward. The rocking back and forth seemed to be working for a moment, and then the vehicle suddenly stopped cold and the spinning wheels half disappeared in the sand.

"Looks like we're digging again," he said as he turned off the engine.

We took turns digging out around the four tires, the sand so soft that the holes we dug nearly collapsed back upon themselves as soon as we dug them. After about 10 minutes of this, we had cleared enough room around the tires that we could start backfilling the holes with stones.

Luckily we were in the bottom of a riverbed, with an ample supply of rocks just a 50 foot walk away. Andrew requested large, flat rocks to wedge between the tires and the sand, in order to build up a sort of ramp to drive out on. There were two places in the riverbed that looked like good sources for these particular types of rocks, so we split up, Ash heading towards the pile to the south and me heading to the pile to the north.

It was exhausting work, hauling those large rocks back to the vehicle, especially after all the digging we had already done. It was also quite hot, being fully exposed in that riverbed, the mid-morning sun reflecting harshly off the pinkish sand.

We needed just a few more stones, so Ash and I headed back to our respective rock piles one last time.

"Elephant!" Ash said suddenly in a very loud whisper, trying to find that sweet spot between saying it loud enough for us to hear it from a distance and not saying it so loud that she disturbed the giant beasts lurking in the bushes a dozen or so yards from her rock pile.

As we were placing what we hoped would finally be the last rocks between the tires and the sand, we heard another noise; a series of deep growls, coming from the opposite side of the river, where I had just been gathering stones.

"Lions!" Andrew said. We all stood there, frozen, for what seemed like a minute or two, listening to the deep growling as it echoed off the banks down the riverbed towards us. It was gradually getting louder. They were getting closer.

"They're in the river bed," Andrew said. "We need to get the hell out of here, NOW!"

Ready or not, our bridge of stone would have to do. Andrew jumped in and started the engine while Ash and I stood by helplessly—the best chance of extracting the vehicle from its sandy prison was to once again keep it light. We watched as Andrew started rocking the vehicle over the rocks, as we constantly glanced over one shoulder for the approaching elephants and then over the other shoulder for the approaching lions.

Andrew was able to get up and out of the holes the vehicle had dug for itself, but quickly ran into another problem: after moving just 15 feet forward, he was starting to get stuck again. Thinking quickly, he jammed the transmission into reverse and floored it, sending the vehicle bouncing violently backwards over the holes we had filled with rock. If he couldn't make it out of this mess going forward, at least he could make it out back the way we had come in.

He flew across the sandy river bottom backwards, hit the ramp we had constructed just half an hour earlier, and was almost up the other side when there was another problem: unable to perfectly control the vehicle in reverse, he wandered slightly off the side of the road and was heading straight for a large tree that would stop him dead in his tracks. He slammed on the brakes, jammed the transmission back into first gear, and headed back out into the sandy river bottom once again in one last desperate attempt to make it up the other side.

In a cloud of pink dust, Andrew once again bounced across the rock-filled holes, the wheels spinning violently as they tried to gain traction at the spot that had nearly trapped him before, and then the vehicle shot up across the opposite bank.

As the dust began to settle and we all high-fived each other, we remembered that we were about to be sandwiched between a herd of elephants and a pride of lions, so Ash and I quickly jumped back in and we all continued on our merry way. As Andrew drove, I reached down for the tracking sheets and bird book on the floor of the vehicle, and had to brush aside half an inch of pink sand to reach them.

Just another day in the bundu.

# A Different Kind of Wild

What is "wilderness"?

In the United States, we have a very specific, legal definition of the term. The Wilderness Act of 1964 (Public Law 88–577) defines wilderness as such:

> "A wilderness, in contrast with those areas where man and his own works dominate the landscape, is hereby recognized as an area where the earth and community of life are untrammeled by man, where man himself is a visitor who does not remain."

The American government defines wilderness as a road-less, car-less area, with no electricity or other modern conveniences. The use of motorized vehicles or other types of mechanized transport devices is strictly prohibited in these legally protected areas.

To many, the United States is looked at as a model for environmental protection and conservation initiatives. Yet if the American idea of wilderness really is to protect places where "man and his own works" do not "dominate the landscape," there is a problem with many of the wilderness areas I've visited in the US. The overwhelming imprints of modern man are well apparent beyond the obvious things like roads, cars, electricity, and buildings. Airplane contrails crisscross the skies during the day, and numerous satellites blaze their trails across that same sky at night. Bridges and other trail improvements have been carefully engineered to make backcountry travel both safe and speedy. And although not nearly as obvious, even the very fabric of the landscape itself has been unmistakably altered.

Everywhere, pristine outdoor wilderness is covered by the heavy fingerprints of man, disguised by a thin veneer of wildness. It's virtually impossible to escape. In countless ways both seen and unseen, the ecosystems we have worked so hard to set aside and maintain as natural have become strange hybrids—part natural, part man-made, struggling for balance all while under the watchful eye of human management. This is the new natural.

-----

In contrast to the American ideal of wilderness, the Tuli Wilderness in eastern Botswana is crisscrossed by roads, traversed daily by vehicles, and features permanent inhabitants who live in a few houses connected to the electrical grid. But the roads that mark the landscape of the Tuli hardly disqualify the area from being referred to as wilderness. I've hiked on trails through wilderness areas in and near Yosemite National Park that are much more eroded and have caused much more significant damage to the natural environment than many of the roads in the Tuli Wilderness have. And while the American wilderness is defined as a place "where man himself is a visitor who does not remain," man has been present in the Tuli Wilderness for probably as long as humans and their immediate ancestors have been on earth. Man is an inextricable part of this wilderness.

In the end, "wilderness" is just a word, used by different people, in different ways, to describe different things. I preferred bundu. The word "bundu." It's a less restrictive definition of wild places, not bound by strict legal mandates. It's more…natural.

Even though the Tuli Wilderness may not be "wilderness" by the American definition, it is one of the wildest places I have ever had the privilege of visiting. I guess that true wilderness is where you find it…

# Be the Bushman

As a child, I kept a brief diary of some of my adventures. On a visit to Yellowstone National Park, sometimes known as the "American Serengeti," when I was nine or ten years old, I carefully logged the wildlife we saw while there:

5 Elk
13 Canadian Geese
3 Deer
2 Buffalo
1 Dead Rat
2 Cranes, One Baby
1 Robin, Nest with Two Eggs
2 Chipmunks
Many Rabbits
4 Moose
1 Marmot
1 Dead Porcupine
Many Mallard Ducks
Many Gulls
Two Lizards

In 1977, about five years later and half a world away in Kruger National Park in South Africa, I wrote this in my diary:

7 Giraffes
10 Warthogs
10 Hippopotami
2 Elephants
25 Baboons

5 Kudu
100's of Impala
3 Cape Hunting Dogs

Clearly this was something in my blood, the tracking of wild game. Then again, maybe it's all just part of the human condition?

-----

Part of the Botswana Conservation and Research Program involved the identification of wildlife, both by direct observation and by inference. You weren't always able to see the animals directly, but you could often tell they had been there by the telltale signs—footprints, scat, etc.—that they left behind. This was the tracking training portion of the program.

With no previous tracking experience, and only two weeks scheduled in the Tuli Wilderness, I was concerned about how much I could learn in such a short amount of time, and if I would be worthy of passing the tracking test—an evaluation one needed to pass before being allowed the privilege to sit in the tracking seat and lead game drives.

About two months before leaving for Botswana, in a failed attempt to prepare myself, I bought a copy of *The Field Guide to Mammals of Southern Africa* and started studying. But other than memorizing the difference between odd-toed ungulates (zebra and rhinoceros—and there are no rhinos left in the Tuli) and even-toed ungulates (everything else on the long list of antelope species in Africa), I was completely lost. I was just looking at what appeared to be random shapes and trying to memorize them. I had no context for what I was looking at; no framework for understanding.

To say that my first day of hands-on tracking instruction in the Tuli was overwhelming would be a gross understatement. We left camp a little before 6 a.m. and less than a quarter mile later Andrew abruptly stopped the vehicle and jumped out. He grabbed a stick from the ground and slowly walked up and down the road ahead of us, looking down at the dirt undisturbed by our vehicle tracks but literally peppered with wildlife tracks, and started circling things. "Right, take a look at these, and once you know what they are, come tell me," he said. Then he walked about 50 feet away and waited.

I squatted down in front of the first set of circled tracks, staring off into space more than at the tracks themselves, and had a minor panic attack. After what seemed like an uncomfortably long time, nothing had come to me. It was time to just start guessing blindly. It was just a few minutes after 6 a.m. on a relatively cool day, and I was already starting to perspire heavily.

Who came up with this ridiculous plan to spend two weeks of "vacation" on a working conservation research program in a remote part of Africa? I could be sitting on a beach somewhere, sipping margaritas and dozing in the warm sun and cool breeze. Whose bright idea was this, anyway?

Oh, that's right. It was mine.

After much embarrassment and grasping at straws on my part, Andrew wouldn't just tell me I was wrong and then identify the track; he would slowly and carefully explain the details, the features that made it unique, and the context for what we were looking at. He would also employ clever mnemonic devices designed to help me (and no doubt himself as well) remember the name of the animal that made a specific track. Then we would jump back in the vehicle and head off down the dirt road again, my overtaxed brain happy for the mental break, my sweaty body glad for the gentle breeze. But before long, my heart would sink once more as he slowed the vehicle to inspect some small, cryptic sign he saw on the surface of the roadway, only to suddenly shut off the engine, jump out, grab another stick, and start circling things again. This would be followed on my end by another minor panic attack, more perspiration, and ultimately more embarrassment as I listened to Andrew slowly and carefully explain why I was wrong.

With time and repetition, and much handholding from Andrew, things suddenly started to fall in to place. I learned how to identify the direction of travel of elephants based on the scuff marks they left in the dirt as they dragged their feet. I learned that an easy way to identify hyena was that their rear pad was turned at a 45 degree angle to the direction of travel, and the difference between brown hyena and spotted hyena tracks is that brown hyena tracks tended to be a lot fuzzier because they had a lot more fur on their feet. I learned that a female Leopard has more pointed toes, where the toes of a male leopard are more rounded and larger. I learned that you can easily tell a civet by the rounded paw, into which you can write the letter "C" between the pad and toes; that you can write the letter "X" between the pad and toes of a black-backed jackal, and that the back pad of a vervet monkey forms the letter "V".

From the tracks of the porcupine, I learned perhaps the most important lesson of all, and that is to step back. If you're having trouble distinguishing between the tracks of a porcupine and a honey badger, which can be somewhat difficult for a novice tracker, step back and look for the obvious: quill marks. It wasn't always just about the shape of the track itself. Looking at the track in a larger context was also very important.

-----

When I was working in the Archaeology Lab at Cal Poly during my undergraduate studies, I remember sorting through countless artifacts from various archaeological sites throughout California and having a hard time determining how to classify many of them. It was easy to tell that a projectile point (commonly referred to as an "arrowhead") was a projectile point; it was much more difficult for me to determine that it was a certain type of projectile point. I watched Professor Blackburn fly through the box of artifacts quickly, identifying the types more quickly than I could even take notes, let alone learn from his descriptions. It wasn't until I discovered something called a "projectile point typology" that I was able to put everything in context.

The projectile point typology grouped like objects together into categories. Not only did each category have a name, but it also had a list of distinguishing features along with it. So with a typology you didn't look at the whole point to determine what type it was; you looked for specific features, which then led you down a path of deductive reasoning to the obvious conclusion that it was a certain type of projectile point. It was a key to understanding the projectile points of a specific site or a region as well as a specific time period.

Once I learned this, not only did it become easy to identify even the most obscure projectile points, but I also started developing new projectile point typologies for archaeological sites that we were inventorying.  Once given the right tools, understanding came easily.

I found myself in a very similar situation with tracking.  Andrew broke down the track into its component parts and taught me that certain features meant certain things.  Rather than trying futilely to memorize entire shapes for specific animals, I was instead able to commit smaller component features to memory. It was not unlike the projectile point typologies that had helped me so much back at Cal Poly.  I was no longer guessing; I was giving informed answers.  They were not always right, but at least they had a logical basis and I was getting closer.

Andrew first taught me the basic difference between dogs and cats—canids have two lobes on their paw, while felids have three—which is one of the first fundamental steps in helping to narrow down the identification of an animal from its tracks.

He also taught me about "registering"—when the front and back tracks of an animal are superimposed, often making it more difficult to identify the species based on the shape of the track alone, it can give you another clue to aid in identification, as only certain species "register."

With these and other tools, the impossible suddenly started to look possible.  I still had a steep mountain to climb, but I could see that there was hope.

I was shown tracks of civet, small spotted genet, large spotted genet, brown hyena, spotted hyena, lion, leopard, porcupine, honey badger, zebra, impala, wildebeest, and many other typical African mammals.  What surprised me most was that it wasn't just about the mammals; it was about <u>everything</u>.  I was also expected to be able to identify the tracks of insects—millipedes, scorpions, different types of ants, termites, "ant lions," etc.—as well as lizards, snakes, tortoises, terrapins, and even birds. The birds were perhaps the most troubling: it's one thing to identify the tracks of something with a pretty unique tracking signature, such as an ostrich or a corey bustard (the world's largest flighted bird); it's an entirely different level of commitment to understand the subtle differences between the many hundreds of smaller birds with nearly identical tracks.

Although I was making progress, Andrew continued to torture me with increasingly difficult challenges. For once, couldn't he just ask me to identify the ubiquitous elephant tracks? Those were easy.

Or were they?

We turned off Mohave Highway onto the lesser road leading out towards The Marsh, and Andrew stopped the vehicle. Here we go again.

He jumped out and drew an elongated circle around a serpentine, linear track. "When you know what it is, come tell me," he said, walking off. I was practically right behind him, because this was such an easy one.

"It's a snake," I said. "Sorry, I don't know exactly which species, but I know it's a big one."

"Wrong," he said. "Try again."

I walked back over to the track, dejected. After pretending to study the track for a while but actually just staring blindly into space, I noticed the many elephant tracks on either side of my supposed snake track. So which came first, the elephants or the unknown snake that wasn't even really a snake? Just as I was about to approach him with another blind guess—monitor lizard, which I already knew was wrong because there were no foot marks—it suddenly dawned on me: this was one of those trick questions that Andrew was famous for.

I ran back over to him and said "It's an elephant dragging its trunk on the ground!"

"Correct!" he said. "Good work!"

But my first real breakthrough came when we were on one of the many dirt roads just outside of Mohave Camp, about 10 to 15 miles northwest of Serolo Camp. Driving along quickly, Andrew suddenly slammed on the brakes and said "Hello!" He jumped out and quickly circled a track. "What's this?" He asked. Rather than walk away like he usually did, he stood over me and waited for a quick response; so rather than suffer in silence like I usually did, I decided to verbalize my thinking process.

"Three lobes," I said, "so it's a felid. Looks too big to be a lion, but it's still a good size. It's not a cheetah, because cheetah's don't have retractable claws, and I don't see any claw marks. So..."

"Good," he said, interrupting me before I could state the obvious conclusion of my line of deductive reasoning. "It's leopard." But he didn't have to say that. He already knew that I knew.

-----

Andrew was a great tracker—an expert. But Johannes was a master. I had seen him in action on my first evening drive in the Tuli, and was blown away not just by his vast knowledge, but also by the calm, cool manner with which he conducted himself. For Johannes, everything seemed easy.

Johannes rides his bike everywhere; he probably rides about 15 miles a day, on dirt roads, and in the oppressive midday heat of the Tuli he never breaks a sweat. It wasn't unusual for Johannes to track both a leopard and a cheetah from his bike at the same time while riding to work at the main office. It was all quite remarkable considering that sightings of leopards, especially in the daytime, were uncommon, and that nobody (except for Johannes) had seen a cheetah in the Tuli Wilderness for more than a year.

Every day Johannes chops wood from dead mopane trunks and branches to fuel the campfire as well as the "donkey boilers," which are used to boil water for the camp. One day he carefully whittled two mopane branches and used them to teach me to make fire. We took turns, one holding the base while the other spun the drill. For a man his age, he was very fast; it was difficult to keep up with him. I soon realized that it wasn't just his speed; it was the efficiency of his movements. There was not a drop of energy wasted in his actions. All of his movements were carefully calculated, focused on the task at hand; just enough energy was expended to accomplish our goal of starting a fire, and not a drop more. After five or ten minutes of exhausting work—mostly by him—a glowing ember appeared in the base. He dumped the ember into a clump of dried elephant dung and started blowing. Before long, smoke and flames were billowing out of the dung. I was never more excited and proud to see a burning pile of shit than I was at that moment.

Johannes could make fire with ease, but it was tracking where he really excelled. It makes perfect sense if you think about the importance of tracking to the Bushman: successfully tracking wildlife meant that they ate, and thus survived; not doing so meant starvation and, ultimately, death.

Andrew was my teacher, but Johannes was my idol. Every chance I got to tag along with him, I spent more time watching his eye movement, his foot placement, and his body language than I did looking at the tracks he was following and the animals he found. From Andrew I learned tracking, but Johannes gave me an insight into the mind of a Bushman, a man completely at one with his surroundings.

I could never be a Bushman. I'm 50 years old and live in a suburb and work in an office half a world away from the Tuli Wilderness. But in many ways, I really needed to be more like a Bushman.

I went to Botswana with no real agenda other than to experience it; to drink it all in. My only real goal while there was to maybe pass the tracking test. Of course, passing the test and being allowed to sit in the tracking seat didn't mean I was anywhere near as qualified as Johannes or Andrew; my knowledge of tracking was probably less than one percent of all that they knew. Being given that honor would signify that I really accomplished something on by trip back to the bundu; that I was not just memorizing shapes out of a book—that I had gained a familiarity with my surroundings and a comfort level with and awareness of the natural environment there.

I wasn't yet, and never really would be, at one with the bundu like Johannes the Bushman, but I was beginning to understand it as well as anyone could on such a short visit.

-----

Just a few days before my stay in the Tuli was over and it was time to return to "civilization," Andrew pulled me aside and said "Matt, I just wanted to let you know that you passed your tracking test. Good job. I'm very impressed with how quickly you picked all of this up."

Say WHAT?

I had really tried to take the mountain of information Andrew was throwing at me seriously, and not just memorize it but understand it. I was elated that all my hard work had been recognized. Now the day had come, and I wondered: was I really worthy?

Later that evening, as we were loading the vehicle for our night drive, Andrew made a formal announcement to the group. "Listen up everyone. I want to tell you all that Matt has passed his tracking test. Because he passed his tracking test, he'll be sitting in the tracking seat on our night drive. This is what you have to look forward to; this is your goal. Work hard on learning your tracks, and maybe before you leave you'll be sitting in this seat."

He motioned for me to mount the tracking seat. It was a glorious moment. On my first night in the Tuli Wilderness I had been blown away by the ease with which Johannes had so skillfully guided us from that very seat. Now it was my turn. Was I even remotely ready for this responsibility—this honor?

It was almost as if I could hear the angels singing; I imagined a glorious halo emanating from the sacred seat as I reached up and accidentally knocked off the spotlight, which immediately fell to the ground and broke.

It was quite an auspicious start to my first night in the tracking seat.

With a few minutes of fiddling with the wiring, Andrew was able to get the spotlight working again. After some quick instructions on how to operate the light, how to scan for animals, how to not blind certain species of antelope, and how to avoid lighting up elephants, we set off towards the Limpopo River.

It was quite exhausting trying to hold on to the flimsy seat with one hand while using the spotlight to scan up, down, and sideways, all while driving on bumpy and rutted dirt roads through overgrown riverine vegetation in the dark. Oh, and the headlights on our vehicle didn't work, so in operating the spotlight I had to simultaneously look for animals and illuminate the rough track in front of us.

We saw lots of various species of antelope, a few spring hares, and a few other miscellaneous creatures. After about fifteen minutes along the river, we turned north and headed back to the roads closer to the main office and Serolo Camp. Scanning to my right on one of these roads, I saw a huge spiked objected trotting away from us and yelled "porcupine!"

It was my first sighting of the African porcupine, and the thing was gigantic. Andrew turned the vehicle off of the road and started following the creature. About a hundred feet off in the bush, the engine started to sputter and die.

"Quick," Andrew yelled, "turn off the light!"

I blundered around and eventually found the switch. But it was too late. The battery was dead.

"Great, Matt!" Andrew said sarcastically. "You've been in the tracking seat for all of fifteen minutes and you've managed to break both the spotlight and the vehicle!"

We had a very nice time sitting in the dark admiring the stars of the Milky Way as we waited about half an hour for Bethule, Johannes, and Christoff to come and jump-start the vehicle. They took the vehicle with the dead battery back to the main office, only about a mile away, while we continued many miles northward on our night drive using their vehicle. We made it back to camp right about midnight, having seen an amazing variety of wildlife, and my arms, shoulders, and neck ached from operating the spotlight all night.

-----

Stories are a very important aspect of our society, and storytelling is one of the things that make us uniquely human. Stories convey important knowledge about the world around us, often in a simplified yet dramatic fashion designed for maximum impact. We have much to learn, remember, and understand in life; wrap a great story around something and it can make an impression on us that lasts a lifetime.

I had read somewhere that tracking is not just about identifying the species; done correctly, it's all about storytelling. I didn't really understand this until one morning when we were driving north along Mohave Highway once again looking for tracks and Andrew saw something unusual.

We passed the turnoff to The Marsh, an area known for its spotted hyenas, and Andrew slowed the vehicle. Hanging half out of the doorless driver's side, he crept along slowly with a puzzled look on his face.

After some time, I asked him "What do you see?"

"I don't know..." It was the first of only two times during my stay in the Tuli Wilderness that Andrew wasn't 100 percent sure what he was looking at.

He eventually stopped and got out for a closer look. He wandered up and down the road for quite a while, stopping from time to time to crouch down and inspect the tracks closer. He got back in the vehicle and we continued driving north. After a few minutes, Andrew stopped the vehicle again. He still saw the strange markings in the sand, and it was really starting to bug him.

This time I got out and followed him. There was a set of spotted hyena tracks, moving southward along Mohave Highway back towards The Marsh. On one side the tracks were two lines, running parallel to the line of travel and twisting in and out of each other, much like the outer walls of a strand of DNA. The mystery lines were on one side of the Hyena tracks for a hundred or so feet, and then abruptly switch to the other side.

"Do you think the hyena has a snare stuck on it, and the lines we're seeing are from the wires dragging on the ground?" I asked.

"No," replied Andrew. "It doesn't look like a snare. I'm thinking it's some kind of vegetation…but it just doesn't make any sense."

"Do you think it could be dragging the body of a dead antelope, and the two lines you see are from the hooves?" I asked?

"No," he replied. "If it was an antelope, even a small one, the hyena's tracks would look different; its legs would be splayed apart more as it struggled under the heavy load."

Still puzzled, we both got back in the vehicle and drove on.

After driving another mile, we were still seeing the mystery tracks in the road, and they were obviously still bugging Andrew. He stopped the vehicle and we got out again.

"I was wrong," he said. "It's carrying an antelope. The two lines are the hoof marks. The reason the hyena's tracks look normal is that it's not carrying the complete animal, just the hind section."

It's from observations like this that Bushmen develop stories. It's not enough to just identify the animal; almost anyone with a cheat sheet of animal tracks and a little knowledge could do that. Real tracking was about understanding all the details; the animal, the circumstances, the time, and the place.

We had deduced that the previous evening, an antelope— possibly a sub-adult impala—had been killed by predators. The spotted hyena had probably heard the kill, and took off towards the sound to see what it could scavenge. It managed to walk off with a small piece of the hind section of the antelope, and used the convenient Mohave Highway to drag the hunk of nourishment the three or so miles back to its den, where its hungry pups were waiting. In doing all of this, it left behind a few cryptic clues in the sand, those clues waiting for someone, maybe a Bushman, or maybe just someone who wanted to be a little bit more like a Bushman, to happen upon them and to uncover this story of life and death in the bundu, before a vehicle drove down the road, the wind kicked up, a herd of elephant walked by, or it started to rain, and the story disappeared forever into the ether.

# Sebatana

It was a relatively slow afternoon as far as animal activity goes. Other than a few impala here and there, and the resident herds of zebra we almost always saw out at Red Plains, we were not seeing a lot of wildlife.

It was so quiet that we stopped to watch a group of helmeted guinea fowl. Four or five of them were huddled by the side of the road, and I snapped off a few photos as they slowly wandered away from us into a grassy opening through the ever-present mopane trees. They seemed a little skittish, as if they were reluctant to move too fast or too far away from us and go out into the opening.

We watched them for a long time; much longer than we would normally give to such a common species. That's the kind of afternoon it was. Sometimes the animals were everywhere. Sometimes they were nowhere.

When we had had more than enough of the guinea fowl, Andrew wrapped his finger around the key in the ignition. Just as he was about to turn the key, Ash said "Wait! Is that the lion?"

Off in the distance, in the fading afternoon light, we could just barely make out the head of a female lion in the tall grass of the opening. And she was moving directly towards us.

Andrew started the vehicle and backed it off of the road into the clearing where the guinea fowl had been just a minute earlier, expertly positioning us for our lion encounter. We turned our heads around to watch the lion, now completely behind us, as it walked closer, and closer, and closer, our heads gradually swiveling around, until there she was, parallel to the vehicle, just 10 to 15 feet away. She seemed to pay no attention to us at all, until she was at her closest point; she kept moving forward, but spun her head to her right side, and she looked me right in the eye.

It was Sebatana!

-----

The lions of the greater Tuli area have suffered mightily at the hands of man. Because the Tuli is mostly unfenced, animals are free to roam in and out of the area at will, as they did for millions of years in the natural landscape, before man came along and mucked everything up. But the protection offered by the Tuli was a loose protection at best; the animals that freely wandered the protected area were equally free to wander into farms, game ranches, and populated areas—the places were where the lions usually met their fate.

Every hunter dreams of shooting an African lion. It's the ultimate trophy; the definitive sign of manliness. And to truly be a man, you need to shoot a male lion. Even though female lions do the vast majority of the hunting for the pride, while the males laze around in the sun all day, napping and looking pretty, no self-respecting hunter wants a female lion. The result: all of the males are shot, while the females roam freely, their individual lives spared, but the overall health of their species in serious jeopardy. Without viable breeding populations, the species will quickly wither and die out.

All of the male lions in the Tuli had been killed in recent years. Just seventeen lions remained in the entire Tuli area, and all of them were female. The lions of Tuli looked to be breathing their last breath.

Then a funny thing happened. Two male lions from neighboring Zimbabwe strayed over the border and spent a couple of months wandering through the Tuli. They encountered a female lion named Sebatana, who with her mother comprised the only lion pride that had made its permanent residence within the borders of the Tuli Wilderness. Three or four months later, with the two roaming males long gone back to their home in Zimbabwe, Sebatana gave birth to three cubs. In a huge stroke of luck for the lion population of the Tuli, all three of the cubs were male.

-----

Sebatana was all alone that afternoon, and she looked tired, trudging along after a long, unsuccessful day of hunting. She walked right past us and onto the dirt road called Sesame Link. She was probably on her way to her cubs. So we followed her.

Her cubs were about a year old now. Recent volunteers had seen just two cubs in Sebatana's pride, and it was unknown if the third one was still alive. As part of the Botswana Conservation and Research Program, we needed to try to find her cubs—first to see if all three of them were still alive, and second to try to get some photographs of them so we could create identification sheets for them.

We followed behind Sebatana as she slowly plodded along Sesame Link until it intersected with Sesame Street, a dirt road that runs along the base of a rocky outcrop known as Bedrock. At the intersection, she kept going straight, into the bush, then up into the rocks, and we quickly lost sight of her in the twilight. Without a road, we couldn't follow her any more.

"I think I know where she's going," Andrew said. He turned left on Sesame Street, which followed the base of Bedrock and eventually curved around and out on to an open plain on the other side. Andrew's assumption was that Sebatana was taking a short cut over the top of Bedrock and would end up on the other side.

Just then, Johann's voice came over the radio. He and Jocelyn were nearby, and they quickly fell in line behind us on Sesame Street, joining the hunt.

When we got to the other side of Bedrock and stood out in the open plain, the light almost gone now, scanning everywhere for any sign of Sebatana and her boys, we quickly realized that we wouldn't be seeing any more of Sebatana that night. She was gone. Counting her cubs and identifying them would have to wait for another day.

Johann and Jocelyn decided to head back to camp. Andrew seemed a little reluctant to give up on the elusive big cat just yet, and he hesitated for a moment.

As Johann pulled away, Jocelyn, concerned about the coming darkness, leaned her head out of the window of the Land Rover.

"The night comes quickly in Africa," she said to Andrew.

"Don't let the night catch you."

# Tree of Life

When I first arrived in the Tuli Wilderness, there was something immediately very familiar about the place. It somehow almost felt like home, but not for the reason you would think. Oh, the African bush looked familiar, even after a 35-year absence. But the comfort I was feeling was not the Africa in my blood. It was something else.

I came to the Tuli from another world; a separate life in California. In California, our landscapes tend to fall in to three broad categories: natural areas, urban and suburban areas, and agricultural areas.

California is well known for its natural areas—wild, iconic protected places such as Yosemite and Death Valley National Parks and countless others. Most residents and visitors are also very familiar with California's large urban and suburban areas such as Los Angeles and San Francisco, which are highly developed and are almost completely devoid of any sense of naturalness. And as the "bread basket" of the United States, California is also well known for its abundant agricultural areas.

Natural areas are beautiful. Urban/suburban areas, not so much. The agricultural areas seem to fall somewhere in between: green, fertile, and open, they are beautiful in an unnaturally natural sort of way, giving modern humans a feeling of the natural world even while they are just as heavily modified by modern man as areas of urban and suburban blight.

While there was nothing natural about completely stripping the landscape of its diverse mix of native plants and animals and replacing it with row after row of carefully manicured monoculture, in a landscape so heavily modified by man, we take our beauty and our nature in any way we can get it. For many of us slaves to modern society, agricultural land is beautiful and "natural" in its own way, and it is the closest thing we have to a natural landscape.

While I find little pleasure in glancing at a field of broccoli or lettuce and trying to imagine the way the landscape looked before it was raped by man, I do find an unnatural beauty in two things that are very familiar to me and well-known features of the California landscape: citrus groves and vineyards. For many people, these neatly cropped, carefully spaced, symmetrically trimmed grape vines and orange trees are a large part of what makes California special.

-----

The two dominant features of the landscape in the Tuli Wilderness in eastern Botswana are mopane trees and elephants. And in this place, the two are inexorably linked.

The leaves of the mopane are shaped like the two wings of a butterfly, connected together at the stem like the body of an insect. In the slightest breeze, these two "wings" begin to flutter, producing a gentle flapping sound while making the trees look as though a thousand or more bright green butterflies might suddenly take flight and rise above the red plains, high into the skies, leaving a vast graveyard of leafless, skeleton-like mopane trees behind. But it's not the leaves taking flight in a slight breeze that strips these trees bare. It's the elephants.

At the end of the rainy season, tall green grass is abundant in the Tuli. The elephants grasp large clumps of it with their trunks and rip them from the ground, then shake the clumps violently back and forth, creating small clouds of red dust as they remove the dirt from the grass before placing it in their mouths and chewing it roughly and loudly.

The abundant annual green grasses don't last long. When the graze is gone, the elephants turn to browsing for their sustenance, and their perennial plant of choice is the mopane tree. To the elephant of the Tuli, the mopane tree is the tree of life.

Elephants are large, lumbering creatures with sensitive foot pads and a massive bulk that needs to be carefully balanced. As such, they prefer flat, open areas of sand and dirt, and tend to avoid areas of hills and rocks. In the landscapes they prefer—the flatter, less rocky areas—the mopane trees are literally mowed down by the elephants.

The effect of the large herds of elephant continually browsing the mopane across the expansive Tuli landscape is practically devastating. Depending on the location and the level of use, the height and spacing of the trimmed mopane trees can vary from several feet tall to a dozen feet or so.

Just like the fields of grape vines and citrus trees back in California.

Just like home...

-----

At the end of another long day, after experiencing yet another vehicle failure in the dark in a remote section of the Tuli Wilderness, we were once again rescued, this time by Johann, who happened to be only a few miles away when we sent out the distress call over the radio. The Land Rover he was driving was already full, so it was a tight squeeze to force me, Ash, Andrew, and all of our gear in. We took over the center seats; Johann and Jocelyn sat in the front, while Anneline moved to the back with her three small children.

Anneline's oldest child, her four-year-old daughter Ruby, was born in the Tuli Wilderness, and knew of no other way of life. She kept herself occupied on the drive back by trying to pluck the ever present mopane leaves from the trees as we drove by. It was all she could talk about. I wasn't sure exactly why she was so passionate about the leaves of this one particular tree. Perhaps it was their likeness to a whimsical butterfly that captured the imagination of a child. Or perhaps as a native of the Tuli, she, like the elephants, had an instinctive sense that this was the tree of life.

"I want some mopane leaves!" she said repeatedly, sticking her hand out of the moving vehicle in the dark. But we were too far away, and we were moving too fast. She would occasionally manage to touch a leaf or two, but with her tiny hands, she wasn't able to successfully grab any.

It was late, and Ruby was tired and hungry after a long day out in the bundu. These things combined with her frustrating attempts to grab mopane leaves eventually moved her to tears.

"I want some mopane leaves!" she cried.

When Ruby started crying about her precious mopane leaves, I felt compelled to do something. Not something "parently." Something "grandparently."

When my children were that age, in a similar situation, I would have told them to simply stop crying. My children were adults now, and I was 50 years old and in a completely different phase of life. Although my wife and I were not yet grandparents, we knew that that experience was probably right around the corner. We were already preparing for it mentally. I guess it's just all part of the circle of life.

I casually stuck my hand out of the window in the dark, and started tapping on leaves of mopane trees close to the passing vehicle. Alas, as they were for Ruby, they were also too far away and moving too quickly for me to grab.

Then I made a plan. In another mile or so, we would be at Red Plains. Just before we got to Red Plains, we would slow considerably where the Mohave Highway dropped into a rutted, muddy, twisting section of the road. On that part of the drive, our vehicle always seemed to be brushing up against some mopane trees that grew practically right on top of the road, their roots no doubt drinking up the life-giving water that always seemed to be collecting in the deep ruts there.

A few minutes later, my assessment proved correct; as Johann maneuvered the vehicle through the muddy ruts, a mopane tree brushed the right side of the vehicle where I was sitting. I stuck my hand out, and a nice bunch of leaves was deposited cleanly into my palm. All I had to do was tighten my fingers and latch on to Ruby's leaves and hold tight. As the vehicle moved forward, the leaves were easily liberated from the branch.

I turned back towards Ruby and extended my hand to her.

"I got you some mopane leaves…"

# Bitchy Old Cow

We sat on our favorite rock under the shade of a large mashatu tree, high on the eastern bank of the Motloutse River, clutching our clip boards and binoculars. From this spot, it wasn't unusual to see three or four herds of elephants come by over the course of an hour. On this morning, we saw three herds in just 15 minutes.

As the first herd poked their tusks out from behind the mopane trees lining the opposite bank of the river, you could see their body language change. They were excited to see the water. Some moved slowly down the steep riverbank, while others trotted quickly; a few of the more playful ones scooted or even rolled their large bodies down the bank. Once down to the river, most spent the entire time drinking as much as they could, while a few played in the water or just rolled in the mud. We counted 16 elephants in that herd.

Just as the herd had had its fill and were starting to move slowly off to the north, another herd came out of the trees. It was much smaller, just four individuals, but they were equally excited to see the water. While they were drinking, more elephants materialized out of the green shrubs and moved down to the sandy pools in the river bottom. This third herd contained a higher percentage of juveniles, and even one baby. It was very difficult to count and sex this herd because the small ones were mostly hidden behind the huge adults. After about 10 minutes of struggling, we came up with a count that we could all agree on: this herd also had 16 elephants in it.

These were the elephants of Tuli. It's comforting to know that at a time in earth's long history when there isn't a lot left that is really natural, it's still possible to witness something so truly wild.

-----

Later that day, we left camp on our afternoon/night drive right about 5 p.m. and headed north on Mohave Highway. Out near the northern end of Red Plains, we saw a herd of elephants off to the west, behind some distant mopane trees. They appeared to be moving slowly towards us as they were eating a mixture of crisp mopane leaves and long grass, and their trajectory would roughly put them about a hundred or so feet in front of us as they crossed the road. We stopped the vehicle on the open plain and waited for them to come out from behind the trees so we could get an accurate count and a description of the composition of the herd to record on the elephant data sheet.

While we were waiting for the elephants to slowly make their way closer to us, we noticed a white truck off to the east, just past the eastern border of the Tuli Wilderness property. It was a group of men from neighboring Talana Farms. They were still on their own property, but they were very close to crossing onto our property, and they had a reputation for being bad neighbors. Perhaps they were planning on shooting one of the numerous zebra or other ungulates that frequented the Red Plains, or maybe they were just out looking to scrounge up some firewood. We didn't know why they were there, but they were acting very suspicious, so we kept a close eye on them.

Andrew got out of our vehicle and started on one of his well-deserved rants about the jerks from Talana. While he was ranting, he asked me to look through my binoculars to see if I could tell what they were up to. Two men were in the cab of the truck, and three more were sitting in the bed. They were moving very slowly and tentatively, stopping frequently, and they were eyeing us closely. But they were not really doing anything that I could see. Their nefarious plans for that evening were probably foiled when they saw the tree-huggers from Tuli roll across the plain in their battered Land Rover to count their stupid elephants.

As Andrew continued with stories of short-sightedness and cruelty at the hands of Talana, the elephant herd behind his back gradually came out of the bush into the open plain and moved slowly towards us. Suddenly a large, mature female appeared from behind one of the taller mopane trees, off to the left side of the rest of the herd. This was a female Andrew knew very well. She was easily recognizable because if she was a human, she would have desperately needed some serious orthodontic work—her right tusk sloped upward, and her left tusk sloped downward. It seems that the red Tuli dust caked to her body was not the only reason her neck looked red.

Andrew knew her as an animal that had never given anyone any trouble before—she was very level-headed and extremely mild-mannered. Except that that evening, she wasn't. As she came out from behind the trees towards us, she was trumpeting loudly, kicking up dirt, and moving quickly. What happened next was a gigantic blur, and I didn't fully understand it until later.

The elephant ran towards us, in what I assumed at the time was a mock charge. Andrew started screaming "Hey! Hey! Hey!" at her as he simultaneously jumped in the vehicle, honked the horn, started the engine, jammed it into reverse, spun the wheels in a cloud of red dust, and took off backwards down the open plain. While this was happening, I was snapping photos of the elephant as quickly as I could, thinking "She's getting really close; these are going to be some great shots!"

The old cow got within 10 to 15 feet of us before she turned off to her right and retreated back around the trees from which she had originally emerged. Further back, where the Red Plains meet the green mopane trees, the rest of the herd had gathered and were huddling close together.

"See what they're doing?" Andrew asked. Ten or more elephants had formed a semi-circle at the edge of the plains. The adults formed the outer edge of the semi-circle, their tusks all facing outwards menacingly. Inside this great wall of elephant flesh were all of the juveniles. "They're in defensive mode now, protecting their family."

Ash had been sitting in the passenger seat of the vehicle, with no door between her and the charging elephant. On several previous occasions she had told me that the only animal she was really afraid of was elephants, so I assumed that this had to have been the most terrifying experience of her life.

As we sat back and watched the herd, she was quiet for a very long time. When she finally spoke, it wasn't at all what I expected.

"It's hard to be angry at an animal that has such a strong sense of family."

Several people in the vehicle started to tear up a little bit. I'm sure it was just all of that red dust in their eyes.

-----

As we watched the errant female eventually rejoin the herd, Andrew explained the difference between a mock charge and a real charge. In a mock charge, the elephant comes at you with its head held low and its trunk extended outwards, but it's all bluster and show—it has no intention of actually following through. I didn't know what I was seeing at the time it happened, but looking back at my photographs, the elephant that came at us that evening was holding her head high and her trunk was neatly tucked under her body. It was clearly a real charge.

"I have no idea why she charged," Andrew said. "And I have no idea why she stopped short."

"Bitchy old cow," he added. "She's probably having a bad day. Maybe PMSing."

Andrew was still trembling and talking in an excited voice 15 minutes after it happened. That's when I started to understand how serious it had been. He had seen it all in Africa, and it took quite a bit to elevate his pulse rate.

Later that evening, after dinner, we talked for quite some time about our encounter with the old bitch out on the Red Plains.

"I seriously thought we were going to get flattened!" Andrew said.

# We Are the Road Crew

"This is dedicated to a fine body of man. It's called 'We Are the Road Crew'."

—Lemmy Kilminster

Roads are the backbone of the Tuli Wilderness. But what exactly is a road? No matter how you define it, the majority of earth's human population would probably scoff at using the term "road" to describe some of the things we drove on in the Tuli Wilderness.

The early European settlers of the greater Tuli area found that the only viable modern use of the land was for raising livestock, and even then it proved to be tough going. After years of struggling, most ranchers in the Tuli turned their holdings into game farms, finding that the business of wildlife tourism was much easier and more lucrative than raising livestock.

The majority of the roads in the Tuli Wilderness were probably first established by the ranchers for accessing their livestock. And many of those roads were probably established on or near game trails; those "highways" used by animals that followed the path of least resistance and were burned into the landscape over the millennia were the obvious place for the humans to later place their own roads.

Once established, a road for humans also becomes an important artery for animal travel as well. This was an important aspect of

129

the Botswana Conservation and Research Project, as we drove the roads each morning and scanned the thousands of fresh animal impressions left in the soft, dusty sand before they were obliterated by the passing of our vehicle.

-----

In some places, the roads we travelled were deeply eroded and barely passable, almost like small, rocky canyons. In others, they were two faint lines in the dirt, hardly visible in the daylight and completely invisible to all but the trained eye at night.

In some places, the roads were nothing more than faint depressions in the tall grass, identified with great difficulty only by carefully scanning the landscape and looking for near indiscernible changes in the height of the vegetation. And sometimes, even though the expert behind the wheel would swear otherwise on his mother's grave, you were certain that there was no road there at all, and that he was just making it up as he drove along.

Some of the roads were little more than a faint path up a rocky outcrop, while others were hard packed red dirt that turned in to long stretches of deep mud after a rain. In some places a road travelled along an area of soft pink sand a foot or two deep, making it look more like you were driving along a dry river bed than a road...because you actually were driving in a dry river bed.

These were the roads of the Tuli Wilderness.

-----

The primary purpose of the Botswana Conservation and Research Project in the Tuli Wilderness is data collection. It's all about the data. And you can't collect data on an area without passable roads; if an area is inaccessible, you collect no data. So out of necessity, a big part of the project was road repair work.

The name of the road we travelled most frequently, Mohave Highway, has to be a pun created by someone with a wicked sense of humor. While it is the major artery running roughly north/south through much of the Tuli Wilderness, it's hardly a highway. Practically the only thing it shares in common with a major highway is that it's mostly straight. Because of its importance in nearly all travel across the Tuli Wilderness, most of our road repair work was concentrated along the Mohave Highway.

We collected rocks—some so close by that they could be carried just a few feet from their resting places; others up to a mile away that we had to haul in to the work area by truck—to fill the ruts and the holes and the divots, and then we backfilled them with shovel full after shovel full of dirt and sand to fill the gaps between the carefully placed stones. It was backbreaking work.

Road maintenance may not be nearly as romantic a task as chasing elephants and lions across the African plain in an open Land Rover, but it's very necessary and highly rewarding. And unlike data collection, the results of your work are instantaneously visible.

-----

A couple of days after a long, hard session of rebuilding Mohave Highway, we headed out in the vehicle with Andrew driving and Johannes in the passenger seat.  Johannes had not been out with us for a few days, so he had not seen the result of all our hard work.

As we passed by one and then another area where we had moved so much rock and dirt to fill a few deep ruts, Johannes looked carefully at the road.  When we passed by a third area that had benefitted from our handiwork, he turned to Andrew and said something in Setswana.

Andrew turned back to the road crew and said, "Johannes says 'good job'."

# A Quiet Evening Stroll

With their low slung hind quarters, powerful front legs, menacing teeth and claws, and a jaw that can snap off a grown man's arm with one bite, hyenas are one of the meanest, nastiest, most efficient killing machines on earth. Hyenas are emblematic of Africa. And our never-ending quest to find the elusive spotted hyena den became emblematic of my stay in the Tuli Wilderness.

Both brown hyena and spotted hyena call the Tuli home. The brown hyena could probably be more appropriately called the shaggy hyena, as it is easily recognizable by its long brown coat. In contrast, the spotted hyena has shorter fur sprinkled with obvious spots. The spotted hyena is a little larger than the brown, and the spotted hyena is also known to be even nastier and more aggressive than its nasty brown cousin.

-----

One afternoon, Andrew asked me if there was anything I had not yet seen that I would like to before leaving in the Tuli.

"Every time we drive up Mohave Highway, I notice 'The Marsh' on the map off to the east," I said. "What is that?"

"Funny you should ask about that," Andrew replied. "I was planning on driving out near there this afternoon to look for the spotted hyena den again."

We had already made several attempts to find the spotted hyena den in a large area of rocks about five miles north of camp. Andrew had seen the hyenas near there with the student group from the UK before I arrived in the Tuli, and was determined to find their den so we could see exactly how many pups there were, what gender they were. If we were lucky, we could even get close enough to take some photos of their spot patterns so we could create identification sheets for them. We had had no luck finding them so far, but we would try again—this time from a different angle.

We drove up Mohave Highway, to the flat spot in the road near Horrible Hill that sits above the rocks where Andrew had seen the hyenas, and where we had spent some time walking through the jumble of rocks looking for them. We drove past that area, down the teeth-chattering and kidney-bruising descent of Horrible Hill, and continued north on Mohave Highway for about a mile before we veered off to the right and onto the road to The Marsh.

Before long, we turned to the right again, onto a small spur that was more of a path than a road, even by Tuli standards, and we stopped near the base of the rocks. Our parking spot was sandwiched between magnificent red rock outcrops on one side, and on the other side a plain that sloped gently down to a low spot about a mile or two off in the distance—The Marsh—that looked to be covered half in low grass and half in water. It was the end of the rainy season, and we had recently experienced some significant showers, so seeing some standing water out there was no surprise.

"There's your marsh," Andrew said. "We can't go all the way. It's still pretty wet out there."

"Do me a favor," he said, "grab your binoculars and tell me if that blue you see out there is water, or is it flowers?"

I pulled the high-powered binoculars out of my pack, put them up tight against my eyes, zoomed all the way in, and carefully focused. There was no standing water out there at all.

"You're right," I said. "Those are blue flowers. I can make out the individual flowers poking out up above the grass."

"There may not be much standing water out there," Andrew said, "but it's still much too wet for us to get too close. So let's take a little walk through these rocks and find the hyena den."

-----

Long past the fear of having my wallet and money and passport stolen out deep in the bundu, I left my backpack sitting on the seat of the open vehicle, taking just my camera with telephoto so that if we were lucky enough to actually find the elusive hyenas this time, I could do my duty and photograph their spot patterns. Ash grabbed her camera, Andrew grabbed his rifle and ten extra bullets, and then we were off. At the last second, I reached back in my pack, grabbed my small video camera, and shoved it in my pocket.

The landscape there was stunning. We scrambled up a ridge which rose above the plain, a flat area of pinkish sand studded here and there with vibrant green mopane trees trimmed down to head-height by the herds of elephants that regularly passed through.

135

The rocky outcrops were red to dark red, in many places stained almost jet black by the elements, and they were mostly undercut, almost giving the impression of gigantic mushrooms rising up out of the landscape. Underneath these dark mushrooms were clear signs that the majority of them had been repeatedly used as hyena dens over the years and were still being used today. Fresh tracks and claw marks, tufts of fur, and an abundance of bones strewn across the ground told us that we were in the right place.

We walked across the ridge, between the rocks, hopped on top of the rocks for a better view, dropped back down between them, and otherwise canvased the ridge, but saw no hyenas. After some time, Andrew whispered that since we were being shut out up in the outcrops we should drop down onto the plain below and see if we could find a hyena or two out there.

The sun had dipped behind the rocks, and everything was bathed in a soft light, a gentle glow that gave off a false sense of peace and tranquility. We started our descent down the outcrop, being careful to be as quiet as possible. About two thirds of the way down to the plain, Ash thought she saw something. Andrew quickly confirmed. It was a spotted hyena, the mother of the pups we were searching for, and she was lying out on the plain about 100 feet from us, between the mopane trees, her head resting on her front paws, eyeing us intently as we attempted to move stealthily down the rocks.

We stopped there and hunkered down, watching closely as the hyena watched us. After about 15 minutes with no movement by us or the hyena, Andrew whispered that we should drop all the way down onto the plain to get a closer look from another angle. So as quietly as possible, we ascended back to the top of the ridge and traversed it north for several hundred yards and found a new spot to drop down to the plain. During our descent, we passed over many more dens that had obviously been used by hyenas in the recent past, but we saw none of the animals there.

When we finally made it out onto the open plain, we scanned to the south, out to where we had seen the mother hyena just a few minutes earlier, but we could not locate her again. We walked a little closer in what we thought was the right direction, constantly moving from side to side in an attempt to see around the mopane trees which were slung low to the ground and formed great cover for predators. And suddenly, there she was.

She was still in the same spot, but as we had moved off to the left about 60 degrees from where we were first watching her, she had obviously been completely aware of our movements and had been tracking us the entire time; in fact, by the time we had noticed her, she was already facing us again. Only this time, we were even closer to her than we had been before; she was now just about 60 feet in front of us.

We squatted down again to watch her. Frozen like a statue, she never broke her stare or moved in any other way.

-----

The light was fading fast, and I wondered how much longer we would be able to safely stay this close to a spotted hyena—and how safe it would have been even in broad light. Andrew was an experienced professional, with a gun; any time a little bit of concern or doubt started to creep into my mind, I would always look towards him for reassurance; after all, he was the master, and I was the student, and I could and should watch him and learn from him. He could teach me many things, and not just the obvious things such as how to correctly identify an animal from the tracks it left behind in the sand; but more subtle things, like how to move in the bush, to not let my fear overcome me, and when I should be concerned.

In one of my brief moments of apprehension that day, we were squatted low to the ground, in a staring contest with a savage predator laying just a stone's throw in front of us, when a terrifying thought struck me:

<u>This was a set up!</u>

This was a mother spotted hyena, with known pups, and she was part of a pack. She was not just a stupid animal; she was a vicious predator with a million years of instinct encoded in her DNA. How many others were out there, watching, waiting, and planning their attack, and where were they? They were probably circling around the back of us right now, ready to lunge in for the kill; the last thing we would hear is them laughing that famously evil hyena laugh as they almost instantly disemboweled us and broke our bodies down into tiny unidentifiable bits, harvesting enough meat off us three humans for a major hyena feast.

As I glanced over to Andrew for comfort once again, I noticed that he wasn't looking in the direction of the hyena any longer. And neither was Ash.

"Do you see that?" Andrew asked.

"Yes," Ash replied.

They were both looking about 45 degrees to the right of the hyena, at the exact same spot on the ridge where we had descended just a few minutes ago.

"Matt, do you see it?" Andrew asked.

"No," I said. "What is it?"

"It's one of the pups," Ash said.

"No, there are two of them," Andrew replied.

"I only see one," Ash responded. "Right there next to that bush."

"Oh," Andrew replied, "I'm looking at two more up in the rocks."

Finally, there were the three pups we had spent so much time looking for. After all of our searching, we had unwittingly almost stepped on them. Now, with the mother watching us closely, two of them were hiding fearfully in the rocks near their den, while the third had a curious eye on us, separated from these interesting humans by only a few low mopane trees and about 30 feet of reddish dirt. Our quiet evening stroll through the rocky outcrops down by The Marsh had just taken on a whole new level of intensity.

"Matt," Andrew whispered, "when the pup turns to the side, make sure to get a good shot or two of the spot pattern so we can identify it later."

Andrew only had to tell me once. I was on it. As the pup moved hesitantly towards us, I zoomed in with my telephoto to the maximum. The pup moved two steps forward, one step back; it moved from side to side; at times it appeared nervous, and then it would stretch, yawn, and lie down. In the rapidly fading light, I knew that it was going to be difficult to get a shot that wasn't blurry and would be useful for identification, so I quickly fired off as many photos as I could.

When the pup got within about 10 feet of us and showed no sign of backing down, my level of anxiety started to increase once again. So I turned on my video camera. At least if this did turn out to be an ambush, people could watch the video later on YouTube and laugh along with the hyenas at our stupidity. Hell, maybe we'd even posthumously win the 2013 Darwin Award for our antics.

"We need to get the hell out of here before it gets too dark," Andrew said suddenly. "And we need to stay as low as possible so as not to threaten them."

As we turned around and started to squat-walk away from the scene, the hyena pup's body language showed an increased level of curiosity. Rather than walk or run away from us as we began to move, the pup started to follow us closely as we made our escape. Each of us took turns looking nervously backwards at the predator trailing us, and our eyes darted around us 360 degrees looking for others that might be coming in to join the hunt. I flopped the video camera loosely back over my shoulder, gathering what I thought might be the last bit of evidence for the inevitable inquiry into the untimely death of the three people who were out for a nice evening stroll and got a little bit too close to the spotted hyena family.

-----

As we walked back towards the vehicle and got a sufficient distance away from the hyena clan, we could once again walk upright and talk above a whisper.

"How was that, Matt?" Andrew asked.

"That was awesome!" I exclaimed.

"I can't believe that just happened!" Ash said.

"That is definitely the closest I have ever been to a spotted hyena on foot!" Andrew said.

It was only then that I noticed that Andrew and Ash were both completely amped up about what we had just witnessed.

"Maybe we shouldn't tell anyone about this…" Andrew said.

-----

The next day, three new volunteers arrived to help out with the Botswana Conservation and Research Project. That evening, as we sat around the table by candlelight after dinner, trying to get to know each other, I found that my new colleagues, like me, had spent substantial amounts of time in Africa—but not nearly as much as Andrew and Ash, who were born and had spent their entire lives and seen so much there.

"You've seen a lot of things out here," one of the new arrivals said to Ash. "What's the most amazing thing you've ever seen?"

"It had to be that spotted hyena pup last night..."

# Improvise

It had already been a long night. As it was a "true" night drive, we had started out late, well after 8 p.m. After experiencing one vehicle breakdown early, we recovered and continued on our journey to the far ends of the Tuli Wilderness, searching for those animal species that only come out at night.

By the time we turned around and started heading home, we were all completely exhausted. Different people handled it differently. One got very quiet. One got grumpy. And one woman simply fell asleep.

Now, falling asleep in a car can be pretty easy. The gentle vibration of the vehicle, the hum of the tires against the pavement, and the plush comfortable seats can make for a rather enjoyable rest. But falling asleep in a Land Rover blazing down the rough dirt roads of the Tuli Wilderness is completely different. Not only does it seem impossible, but it can be downright dangerous.

She probably wasn't used to staying up past 9 p.m. By 9:30, she was fading fast. Her head started to bob, punctuated by the bouncing of the Land Rover over deep ruts in the road, her head coming dangerously close to slamming into the thick metal grab bar in front of her. When she wasn't coming perilously close to knocking herself unconscious, she was almost flying out the side of the vehicle as she drifted off to sleep and her death grip on the grab bar loosened. After two hours of this perverse comedy, she had somehow managed to stay in the vehicle and not receive a concussion.

About 11 p.m., deep in the Tuli, we turned around and started the long drive back to camp. Things were going well until, about a mile from Mohave Camp, the engine started to sputter.

"Shit," Andrew said. "I think we're running out of fuel."

He didn't really have to say it. We knew the sound. We knew the feel. We'd been in this situation before. This wasn't our first rodeo.

He floored the accelerator, trying to keep the engine running up a short hill. The engine sputtered and died, and then he waited a minute and started it again. Flooring the accelerator, he managed to get another 50 to 100 feet of road behind us before stalling out again. He repeated this process for as long as he could. When even the fumes were gone, he got out of the disabled vehicle and called for help.

Nobody was answering the radio this late, and he couldn't get a cell signal from where we were.

"I think if we can all just push the vehicle up to the top of this little hill, I might be able to get a signal up there."

So we got out and pushed. Some reluctantly, others happily. Some were not at all excited to be woken from their slumber, or just were not too happy with being asked to do manual labor of any sort, at any place, at any time. Meanwhile, nobody could see my ear to ear grin in the dark. My time in the Tuli was winding down, and I was relishing every experience. What would happen next? Would we be rescued quickly and back in our plush tents within the hour? Or would we be sleeping out in the open tonight, with no sleeping bags or even warm clothing, forced to stand around a fire all night for warmth while keeping watch for dangerous predators? I was smiling because I didn't care about the answers to any of those questions. It just didn't matter. Nothing really mattered. Whatever happened that night would happen. I was just the guy sitting in a front row seat, enjoying the show.

-----

My previous experience in pushing the Land Rover up a steep rocky road in the Tuli Wilderness had been quite different, as there were only three of us that time—and one of us had to steer. This time, the hill was steeper, but there were seven of us. It was much easier, except that it was pitch black out. The only illumination came from our headlamps, which attracted hundreds of bugs to our faces. I don't have a problem pushing hard and breathing heavily, but swallowing half a dozen African bugs of unknown species was a little disconcerting. And no, they didn't taste like chicken.

Finally at the top of the hill, Andrew was able to get a weak signal on his cell phone and call back to the main office near Serolo Camp. Anneline answered, and said she would send Bethule out immediately with a can of fuel.

Then we waited.

Standing around with our headlamps shut off, the bugs were much less voracious, and the stars were spectacular. As the sweat from pushing the vehicle evaporated and my pulse rate returned to normal, I could see that it was probably going to be a chilly night out.  Good thing that Bethule was already on his way to rescue us.

While we were standing around trying to make the best of the situation, Andrew was thinking.  He was always thinking.  "Always have a plan," the African saying goes.  Well, we had a plan; push the vehicle to the top of the hill and call for help.  Andrew's plan had worked famously, so far.  But in his mind, that was not enough.  In its truest sense, "Always have a plan" also means "Always have a plan B."  Because this was Africa, where you always had a plan, and your plan always changed.

"We're pretty close to Mohave Camp," Andrew said.  "And if we could just push the vehicle up these next two little hills, about half a kilometer, we could just coast the rest of the way in to Mohave Camp.  There's an old generator just outside of the camp, and if we're lucky there might be a few liters of fuel left in the tank.  We could siphon it out, put it in our vehicle, and it would probably be enough to get us about halfway back to camp.  We'll probably even run in to Bethule on Mohave Highway before we run out of fuel again."

What an awesome plan, I thought.  Pure genius.  Some, including me, immediately jumped in to action.  Others hemmed, hawed, sighed, groaned, drug their feet, and reluctantly joined in.

It was a long, strenuous push.  There was more sweat, and lots of heavy breathing.  Several more African mystery bugs were swallowed, and a few tears were shed.  After about 15 minutes of hard pushing, we made it to the top of the last hill.

"Jump in!" Andrew yelled as we crested the hill and, not wanting to lose the slightest bit of momentum, he kept going, accelerating down the hill, as bodies grabbed the sides of the Land Rover in the dark and tried desperately to scramble aboard the fleeing vehicle.

-----

In no time at all, we were on the outskirts of Mohave Camp. Johannes siphoned the fuel out of the generator and into an empty gas can he found nearby. The result was just a paltry one or two liters; not nearly enough to get us home, but enough to get us a few miles closer to Bethule and to rescue. Johannes found an old plastic soda bottle and cut the bottom off of it with his pocket knife, making an improvised funnel. He and Andrew then carefully poured the precious liquid into the vehicle, and we were ready to go.

"Hang on!" Andrew yelled to us. His plan was to get the vehicle up to speed as quickly as possible, and then to try to maintain that speed for as long as possible. This meant that, for all but the deepest ruts and tightest turns, he would be travelling much faster than normal, and every bump and twist and jolt would be amplified tenfold. We were in for a fast, rough ride.

Andrew milked the meager fuel supply like the master that he was. With every minute that passed, I was amazed at how far we had gone, and that we still had not seen Bethule yet. At any moment, we would once again hear that familiar high pitch screaming of the fuel pump, the engine would start to sputter, and we would again be left standing next to the dead vehicle, in the dark, staring at the Milky Way and the Southern Cross and all the other magnificent features on display in the African night sky.

But that never happened. We never ran in to Bethule. And just as the fuel pump started to whine a little bit and the engine began to sputter slightly, a welcome sight appeared in front of the spotlight; that familiar sign with the white letters on the dark brown background:

"Serolo Camp."

-----

Walking back to my tent sometime after midnight, I could barely keep my eyes open. My entire body ached. All I wanted to do was crawl in to bed and pass out. And there on the steps in front of my tent, welcoming me home for the evening, was a representative from the Tuli Chamber of Commerce: *Parabuthus transvaalicus*, the fat-tailed scorpion. It was the species Andrew had warned me about. I walked carefully around it, opened the flap of my tent, and collapsed onto my bed.

I still had a few days left, but I was already starting to miss this place.

# They'll Never Know What Happened to Me....

Andrew was always impressed with my map reading and navigational skills—so much so that his stated goal was to one day get me lost. Or if not lost, at least disoriented.

We headed out to a section of the Tuli Wilderness on the western edge of the property, which gave him the opportunity to get me lost on roads in an area I had not yet had the chance to become familiar with. And I use the term "roads" loosely; like many of the faint lines crisscrossing the Tuli landscape over which we tried to trace the path of our vehicle, this one was in places fairly well-defined and well-eroded, while in other places the only reason you would think there might actually be a road there was because Andrew was familiar with the area and supposedly knew where he was going.

It was a relatively leisurely morning of tracking elephants—the kind of morning where you see what you think is a large rock or termite mound almost completely hidden behind the mopane trees and you are about to just drive on by, and then you notice slight movement so you stop to watch; upon further inspection, you would determine that the object was actually an elephant, so you would get out the map and the elephant data sheet and start writing down information such as date, time, location, gender, direction of movement, mood, activity, etc. Just as you finished filling out the data sheet with a description of the "lone bull" and were about to drive on, another movement in the trees would catch your eye, and you would start to adjust the data sheet to read two elephants; then another movement followed by another adjustment, and so on, until after half an hour of collecting and adjusting data you would finally leave the area, having seen a herd of 20 or so elephants.

Looping back from our far western adventure, we took another road that was new to me, a seemingly nondescript pathway that was to connect us back to one of the main dirt arteries in the Tuli Wilderness. The landscape was peppered with mopane trees, but in this area the trees looked more like bushes, cut down to an average height of about 5 to 6 feet by the constantly-browsing herds of elephant—a truly monotonous scene only occasionally broken up by a single tall, lonely tree of a variety that did not appeal to the discriminating elephant palette.

As we approached one of these randomly-placed larger trees, Andrew slowed the vehicle, and then turned off the engine and coasted to a stop. This typically meant that he had seen something and wanted to approach it quietly, and it was most likely elephant. I quickly scanned the area to the right of the vehicle, where he had been looking the entire time. I looked high and low, close and far, then doubled back with my eyes and did it all again, but saw nothing. His eyes were fixed in a single location, behind the large tree, and he had a strange look on his face. I tried to follow his gaze, but could see nothing in the direction he was looking. He was also oddly quiet.

I decided to break the silence and ask in a whisper what he saw. But before I could speak the words, he said loudly and gruffly:

"Get out."

So I climbed out of the vehicle, unsure of what was happening, assuming that this stop was not about an animal sighting, but about tracks or other signs he had seen.

Once I was out of the vehicle, he said "Walk slowly towards that tree. And don't look at me."

Things were now getting a little strange.

As I followed his instructions and walked slowly towards the tree, being careful not to look at him, I was able to see him acting suspiciously out of the corner of my eye as he slowly removed his rifle from the case and started to follow me.

And that's when it hit me.

Andrew was going to kill me.

-----

We were at least 10 miles from another human being. Nobody would ever find the body. By the time anyone even noticed that I was missing, the hyenas and the jackals and the other scavengers would have picked the site clean of anything that could have been used to identify me or how I had died. The only witness was Ash, who was no help; she would certainly refuse to testify against the love of her life in a court of law.

My panic lasted only a few seconds, as I walked slowly towards my execution. Suddenly I felt a strange sense of calm wash over me, and I was at peace with the world. I even remember having a smile on my face. So, this is how it was going to end, I thought. It's been a long, interesting 50-year ride. Why fight it? Everybody's got to go, sooner or later. You couldn't pick a more beautiful place to die.

With that last thought, I started to glance around at my surroundings, to take in all the beauty of the world for one last time, forgetting about Andrew's instructions not to look at him. "Don't look at me," he barked again. And then, "Don't walk too close to the tree. OK, stop there. Now look in the other direction."

The bullet would probably come soon.

Would he have anything to say to me before pulling the trigger? A simple explanation of why he was doing this to me would be nice, but at this point did it even matter?

Would he ask me if I had any last words?

Would he give me a warning, or just surprise me with the gunshot?

Would the shot come to the back, or to the head?

Would it be one bullet, or two, or many?

Would he get it done quickly? Or was he planning to watch me suffer?

I had so many questions; before much longer, they would all be answered. As my life began to flash before my eyes, my only regret was that I would never get to see my family again, and that they'd never know what happened to me. At least they would know I died doing something I loved — out in nature, exploring, helping with wildlife conservation, in the wilds of Africa.

"Don't watch me as I go behind this tree," Andrew then said as he disappeared.

Wait a minute; was that what this was really about? He's not going to kill me; he just needs to take a piss?

Andrew fumbled in the bushes behind the tree for a minute or two, and then emerged with a big smile on his face, carrying a 20- to 25-pound elephant tusk.

-----

The poaching of elephants for their ivory has long been a problem in Africa and Asia, but in recent years the poachers have seemed to focus their attention more on rhinos than elephants.  There are probably multiple reasons for this. Elephants have retreated to more isolated, protected areas, and it's more difficult than ever to sell their ivory. Meanwhile, rhino horn has a second imaginary medicinal use now: not only is it a cure for impotence, but also now it seems that it is a cure for cancer. Rhino horn on the black market today is more valuable per ounce than gold.

Andrew passed the elephant tusk to me. It was surprisingly heavy, and it was well weathered; this elephant had died of natural causes in an area so remote that it was a long time before someone ran across the tusk. And that someone was Andrew.

How did he find it? He was just out wandering around in the Tuli Wilderness and stumbled across it. This was just one of three tusks he had found over the course of about a year.

"What's the value of a tusk this size?" I asked. He thought for a long time, and then said "A hunter would easily pay $3,000 to $4,000 for this tusk." But in today's atmosphere of sanctions, anti-poaching enforcement, sting operations, and heavy fines (or worse) for those who are caught, many poachers wouldn't even bother trying to kill an elephant for its tusks. "So what would they do if they found it lying on the ground, like you did?" I asked him. "They'd probably take it to a safe place and bury it," he replied, "hoping that in the next five or ten years things change enough that it would be a little easier to sell."

Andrew took a photograph of me holding the tusk, then grabbed it and walked back towards the tree.

"Turn around," he ordered one last time. "I don't want you to see my secret hiding place."

-----

As we drove back towards camp, I tried, as always, to find out exactly where we were on the map. After figuring out our location with about 90 percent certainty, I pointed to a place on the map and asked "So, we're right here on the connector road?"

"Are you kidding?" he replied. "This is the one time when I'm not going to tell you where we are!"

"Do you seriously think I'm going to come all the way back out here someday—without you—and steal that elephant tusk?"

"You never know…"

# Throne of the Ancients

I had come back to the bundu to get closer to nature, and I had certainly seen a lot of nature on my adventure. What I wasn't expecting was that it was also very much about people. And nowhere did I see that more than when we hiked to the top of Eagle Rock.

We left early, driving up Mohave Highway and then wending through a twisted set of roads that on the map looked like a plateful of spaghetti. We eventually reached a place called Eagle Junction, and parked in the parking lot under a tree. Except that it wasn't a parking lot, it was just an area where vehicles had occasionally parked before, where the grass had been beaten down ever so slightly compared to the taller, undisturbed grass next to it. And the lone tree was hardly majestic; not big enough to provide even the slightest bit of shade for the vehicle, it acted more as a signpost saying "Park Here" than anything else.

Andrew grabbed his rifle and walked out on the trail for a few hundred yards, checking for animals, while we stayed back at the parking area. After about five minutes, he reemerged from behind a small rise and told us to follow him.

We hiked along the rocky trail, stopping here and there to identify tracks, scat, and animal remains, before the path dropped down into a little valley below the outcrop that dominated the northern skyline. After crossing a dry stream that had seen water fairly recently, we emerged on a beautiful plain covered with pastel yellow flowers, scaring off a few baboons who loved to eat them. Before long, we were at the base of the rocky outcrop, and then ascended a steep path up to the southern ridge.

Once on the ridge, we followed a faint path that moved east, towards the highest point—Eagle Rock, a prominent feature I had seen every day in the Tuli from a distance of many miles. We passed a large baboon skull, stopped to investigate a massive pair of male kudu horns that had to be at least four, maybe five feet tall, and followed fresh leopard tracks up the trail. Near the top, in a steep, rocky section that seemed to be accessible by only the smallest, most agile species, we paused while Andrew pointed to some large gashes on the bark of an isolated tree. An elephant had been here, and had partially scraped the bark away with its tusks. How an elephant had come this far up—and why it came this far—was a mystery.

Shortly after the elephant markings, we emerged out on a large, rocky plateau, the east side of which drops several hundred feet straight down to the Motloutse River. This was Eagle Rock, possibly the most scenic spot ever in an area already known for its stunning beauty.

Off in the distance, across the river and in the mopane trees a mile or two away, we could see a lone bull elephant browsing. To the right, on the plain below, a large herd of impala and a good-sized herd of kudu lazed comfortably near each other, some slowly grazing on the tall, fresh grass, but most just lying down and resting. Directly below our feet, many colorful lizards came close to see what we were doing and to see if they could scrounge any scraps of food from us. Far below, on the rocks next to the river, a family of rock hyrax nimbly jumped from boulder to boulder. Above our heads, catching the strong updrafts caused by the abrupt rise of Eagle Rock, several birds of prey circled and dove and circled again.

Andrew suggested we each find a nice private spot where we could sit quietly, enjoy the view, and reflect on everything we had seen and everything we had done. The group quickly dispersed across the rocky plateau, which was large enough for everyone to have their own personal space.

Different people in the group did different things. Some sat quietly and never moved a muscle, just taking in the majestic landscape unfolding before them. Others moved around a little more, taking photos of the views and the wildlife. Inexplicably, one person sat with their back to the incredible view, staring sullenly at their boots on the rocks. Oh, well. To each his (or her) own, I suppose. Each person has a different experience, and takes away different things from that experience.

-----

After about half an hour of reflection, Andrew reassembled the group.

"We have a choice on the hike back down," he said. "We can take the faster way. Or we can take the longer, more beautiful way."

One in our party immediately jumped in and voted for the shorter way. As the rest of us started to speak up and vote for the "longer, more beautiful way," it was clear that Andrew never had any intention on taking us the shorter, faster way back. We were in no hurry to get back to camp. We were taking the scenic route.

While our hike up had been confined to the southern side of the ridge, our hike back down skirted around the northern side. This side was less rocky, with more vegetation. There was no real trail here, and it was, as Andrew had promised, even prettier than the hike up had been.

Not too far in to our cross-country hike around the northern ridge, I noticed something peculiar. The ever-present rocks that peppered the landscape looked different here. My intuition told me what they were, but my brain dismissed this explanation as impossible. So I rationalized that the small piles and stacks of rocks in odd places on the hills must have been deposited there by water running off of the top of Eagle Rock.

A minute or two later, Andrew stopped us.

"Does anyone notice anything different in this area?" he asked the group.

I gave the others a brief chance to respond, but the archaeologist in me could hardly hold back my answer.

"Stone walls?" I said, pointing to the unnatural-looking features in the landscape.

"Yes," he answered.

We moved on, climbing a hundred feet or so up a small rise, emerging on a grassy plateau that was literally surrounded by rock—on one side by a large natural wall, and on all other sides by the remnants of man-made walls.

Within the enclosed grassy area were four or five odd-looking piles of rock. Andrew pointed at the closest pile.

"Does anyone know what this is?" he asked.

"A grave?" I replied.

"Yes. This is an ancient settlement. And these are the graves of their chiefs. Once a year, the tribal elders still come here to pay their respects to their ancestors."

The settlement was probably between 500 and 1,000 years old. By taking advantage of natural features of the rocky landscape and then building a series of stone walls to complete the enclosure, they had efficiently built a small fort that was very defensible against attacks by animals as well as by other tribes. And it was just a short walk to the top of Eagle Rock, where they had the best view in the land.

Beneath our feet, the ground was a different color within the walls of the settlement. The typical reddish soil so common elsewhere in the landscape had in this place taken on a distinct whitish tint. Upon closer inspection, the white color was caused by millions of tiny bone fragments that had been mixed into the soil over hundreds of years of occupation. These ancients were obviously meat eaters, which is not surprising considering the prodigious bounty of wildlife that roamed not far beneath their lofty perch, easily spotted from miles away from the top of Eagle Rock.

Andrew went behind a rock and pulled out some special artifacts that helped us understand a little bit more about the people who had lived there. These were not primitive people making simple stone tools; three pieces of iron—an unformed scrap of metal; a wide, flat spear point; and a long, exquisitely crafted barbed arrowhead—were a testament to how advanced these people were. He then showed us a small, delicate bead, finely crafted out of ostrich shell. Together these pieces gave us a small peek into their world; hardly enough to define their existence, but enough to give us a better appreciation for those hearty and resourceful souls who used to call this beautiful place home.

-----

After leaving this throne of the ancients, we continued our journey down the ridge, taking yet another detour. Andrew was looking for a brown hyena den he had seen in this area a year ago, and we needed to find out if it was still in use.

We wandered up several side canyons, boxed in by red rock cliffs, large trees gripping desperately at the steep canyon walls with twisted root systems that looked like something straight out of a fantasy movie. In a place where I had seen so much beauty, and on a day where I had already been completely blown away by the landscape, it just seemed that with every step we took, every corner we rounded, every hill we topped, we saw something even more spectacular. I was beginning to wonder how much more of this my brain could take before it exploded from an overdose of visual stimulation.

Andrew eventually found the brown hyena den in some rocks against a cliff hanging above a small plain. As we walked up to the mouth of the den, walking single file behind him, he saw one of the hyenas dash into the den, but the rest of us did not see it.

So we decided to stand around and wait for a little while to see if it would come back out.

As I stood there waiting for the elusive hyena to emerge, a gentle, misty rain began to fall and I stared not at the opening to the den, but at the ground beneath my feet. The ground around the opening was littered with skulls, horns, teeth, tufts of fur, and bones of all shapes and sizes. Maybe it was just having come from the ancient settlement site high on Eagle Rock just an hour or two earlier, but for some reason I was suddenly struck by the resemblance of the hyena den to a rock shelter—a prehistoric home where early man would have spent his days.

At the opening of a small rock shelter against a cliff edge...

...elevated with a view of the surrounding rocky red hills and plains, ideally situated for spotting prey and defending against other predators...

...a small landing in front of the cliff making a perfect place to return from the hunt and gorge on the spoils...

...the rocks below littered with the debris from a thousand previous hunts...

...deep in the wilds of Africa.

After all of my studying of and fascination with ancient peoples, for the first time in my life, it was as if I was actually experiencing it.

<u>This is exactly what it must have been like</u>.

It mattered little if it was the home of a brown hyena in 2013, or the home of *australopithecus robustus* a million or two years earlier. Man and his ancestors are just a few of the many species of animals to ever inhabit the planet, and we really aren't that different from each other.

# Hunting the Hunters

I was so excited that I could hardly sleep that night. In the morning we would be on anti-poaching patrol, finally going up to the northern fence of the Tuli Wilderness, an area where we would be looking for and removing snares.

It was still dark as I made my way down to the kitchen area the next morning. After chewing down two dry pieces of Weetabix softened by a little cold tea, I did the same thing that I did almost every morning at Serolo Camp: I stood overlooking the watering hole, listening to the birds and the baboons and the monkeys, watching the landscape become slowly illuminated as the sun rose, waiting for the others to come down and have breakfast so that we could start another exciting day exploring the bundu.

Why was I so excited about looking for snares? It's just one of the many ways volunteers with the Botswana Conservation and Research Project occupied their time. But like the road repair work we also did there, there's something so immediately gratifying about pulling snares. When you're collecting data on elephants or other animals, over a long period of time that data builds up into a body of work that can then be leveraged by researchers to learn more about how and where the animals in the Tuli live—and ultimately how to protect them. But when you remove a snare, you instantly and directly save the life of an animal.

We had planned for several days running to head up north on anti-poaching patrol, but had been turned back repeatedly by poor road conditions after the rains. After a couple days of no rain, it looked to finally be the day.

Andrew came out to load the vehicle and seemed to be in quite a hurry. I started walking towards him with my gear, ready to finally get going, when he said to me excitedly, "Matt, today is not the day to forget your camera!" Then he started the vehicle and drove off by himself.

Ten or fifteen minutes later, he was back, having picked up Johannes from the main office. What was going on here?

"Change of plans," he told us. "One of the staff saw a cheetah on the way to work this morning. Johannes is going to help us find it."

-----

Driving out towards the main road, about a mile from our camp, we passed by two local women dressed in traditional clothing gathering firewood. They had collected a large pile of downed and dry mopane branches and had bundled them up, and were taking a short break before attempting to balance their improbable loads on their heads and carry them away. We all smiled and waved to them and said good morning, assuming they were staff we had just not had the pleasure of meeting yet, and drove on by.

About a hundred yards beyond, Andrew turned to Johannes and asked "New staff?"

"No," Johannes replied. "Talana."

166

Andrew slammed on the brakes, got out of the vehicle, and marched back to the two women.

"You are on my property," he said repeatedly. "You are trespassing." After a long, uncomfortable, mostly one-way conversation, he returned to the vehicle, obviously upset.

"They're from Talana," he said, referring to the large agricultural operation that shared a border with the Tuli Wilderness. Talana Farms had a track record of being a bad neighbor, more interested in profits than in conservation. Ironically, on a day that was supposed to be consumed with anti-poaching activities but had changed at the last minute into the hunt for a cheetah, we had stumbled across our first two "poachers," and they were two women that Talana Farms had been sent deep into the Tuli Wilderness to poach firewood.

"Next time..." Johannes said as we drove off, and he then held his two wrists together as if they were joined by handcuffs.

-----

Continuing on, we reached the top of the ridge and parked the vehicle. From here, we would track the cheetah on foot. Andrew grabbed his gun, we all grabbed our cameras, and then we set off down the hill towards the wide open plain. We hadn't walked more than 20 feet when Johannes picked up the tracks.

"Not cheetah," he said. "Leopard."

Andrew and Johannes both chuckled a little at the expense of the junior staff member who couldn't tell the difference between a cheetah and a leopard. But we weren't about to turn around and call it a day. Be it lion, leopard, or cheetah, it was a large predator, and one of the two pillars of the Botswana Conservation and Research Progress was collecting data about large predators.

We continued on, Johannes in the lead, across the plain on a rough trail, and then dropped down into a sandy wash. The leopard tracks continued north through the wash for a few hundred yards before heading east up into a rocky outcrop. We climbed up the steep rocks, eventually reaching a flat plateau on top. It was about 9 a.m., maybe 9:30, and it was already getting very hot.

Johannes looked at the tracks below his feet, then looked out across the plain, towards the next rocky outcrop, which stood about a quarter mile away from us to the northeast, and then looked back down towards his feet.

"Half an hour," he said, referring to the freshness of the tracks beneath us.

"Gone now," he said, lifting his gaze up and across the plain towards the next set of rocks. "Over there. Sleeping."

The leopard had been here half an hour ago, but had already moved on to the next rocky outcrop, finding a cool, shady spot to bed down as the heat of the day picked up. We weren't going to find it now. No matter. We hiked back to the vehicle and drove back to camp. But the morning was far from a complete waste of time and effort. In tracking and <u>not</u> finding that leopard that morning, I had probably learned more from Johannes than I would have had we actually found the animal.

168

An early arrival back at camp after our morning outing gave us the opportunity for a nice long rest. We would leave again in the early afternoon, once again trying for the northern boundary to hunt for snares, unless something else came about to change our plans, as seemed to happen with such regularity in the bundu.

The group reconvened at about 3 p.m. and we set out for what would certainly be a long afternoon and evening. As we drove north on Mohave Highway that afternoon, still stinging from our encounter with the firewood poachers from Talana earlier that day, Andrew stopped the vehicle on the bluff above Horrible Hill and turned off the engine.

He pointed to the northeast, towards the border between the Tuli Wilderness and Talana Farms. Most borders are just imaginary lines that appear on maps, representing the human tendency to arbitrarily divide and classify the land. Borders are lines that mean so much to people, and yet mean so little, if anything at all, to the birds, to the animals, to the trees, and to the landscape. But in the case of the border between the Tuli Wilderness and Talana Farms, this was no imaginary line that existed only on a piece of paper; you could actually see it with your own eyes, from several miles away. It was shocking.

From this scenic viewpoint you could quite easily see the exact location where the ownership of the property changed, just by the changes in the vegetation. "They're destroying their own land for firewood," Andrew said of Talana Farms, "whereas you can see that the Tuli Wilderness is a much more natural landscape."

Since they had basically removed all of the wood from their own property, it was no wonder that they were now sending their staff to come into the Tuli Wilderness to feed their appetite for flames.

-----

We had heard other stories about Talana Farms, the most disturbing of which involved the local pack of African wild dogs. Between habitat loss, poaching, and conflicts with farmers, wild dogs are one of the most threatened species across all of Africa. The pack whose territorial range included both the Tuli Wilderness and Talana Farms met an untimely end at the hands of the local farmer.

One of the things that Talana Farms does is raise ostriches in large pens, like feathered cattle. When the dogs started killing his ostriches and thus threatening his livelihood, the farmer took matters into his own hands and chased down the pack with his truck, killing most of them. He finished off the rest of the pack with poison. And the last pack of African wild dogs in the Tuli became just another statistic.

Or maybe not quite yet.

"Do you hear that?" Andrew asked one night after dinner as we were leaving the campfire and heading back to our tents. There was a sound off in the distance, almost completely drowned out by the cacophony of wildness one hears in the African night. But Andrew had the skill to pick it out and separate it from the background noise with ease.

"Wild dog!"

-----

We drove for a long time to reach the northern boundary of the Tuli Wilderness.  Road conditions had improved significantly due to the lack of rain for a few days and the brutal heat of the midday sun, but there were still plenty of spots where we had to use some caution while driving.

One stretch of Motlhabaneng Road, only a few miles short of our final destination, was particularly troublesome: a low spot in the road where water naturally collected, about 50 yards long, had been heavily trampled by multiple herds of elephants and at first looked impassable.  Andrew stopped and got out for a closer look, walking back and forth along this section multiple times, pressing a foot into the deep mud here and there to judge its strength, before finally deciding that we would go for it.

"Hold on!" he said as he gunned the engine and we went full bore towards the elongated mud hole.  As we began to spin sideways and thick globs of red mud flew all over the vehicle and its passengers, Andrew pitched the right side of vehicle up and off the lip of the road, where he gained just enough traction to power us through to the end of the muddy part without incident.

The rest of the drive was about as uneventful as a drive through the wilds of Africa can be, as we passed jaw dropping scenery, countless animals, and the occasional elephant skeleton or two littering the side of the road.  Before long, we stopped at a junction about a quarter mile short of the boundary fence.  From here we would be continuing our journey on foot. Andrew grabbed his rifle and his spare ammunition.

As we started to walk up the wash to the left, Andrew explained the technique we would be employing. "Animals use these washes as natural pathways," he said, "and there are a number of trails that feed into these washes. This is where poachers tend to set their snares. So we'll walk up this wash for a while, scanning both sides, and looking for wires hanging from the trees, especially around the network of trails you see feeding into the wash."

-----

My first and only previous experience with snares had been on a trail near my house on the slopes of Mt. Hymettus north of Athens, Greece back in the summer of 1978. We had just moved there from South Africa a few weeks earlier, and I was anxious to get back on the trail to further my exploration of the outdoors that I had so fallen in love with during my time down in Africa.

It was a short walk from my house to the edge of my new playground. A well-worn trail cut from the side of the last paved road up into the hills. Whether or not it went up towards the summit of Mt. Hymettus, I didn't know, and likewise didn't care. I would find the way.

I eagerly jumped on the trail, walking way too fast for so early into the hike, unable to contain my excitement. The trail was well-groomed, and the thick aroma of wild Greek herbs filled the air. And less than 50 yards from the point where the trail left the paved road, I fell flat on my face in the middle of the trail, figuratively scratching my head, wondering what the hell had just happened.

It took me a few seconds to assess my surroundings. Attempting to stand up, my left foot would not move more than a few inches. There was a large piece of metal wire wrapped around it and attached firmly to a large herbaceous bush next to the trail. Then it hit me. I was caught in a snare!

Extricating myself from the trap and moving away from the embarrassing scene as quickly as possible, my pace on the trail was even healthier than before, and then—bang. I once again found myself face down in the dirt.

Two minutes into my hike, and I had already been caught twice. Now I was really pissed off. I removed my foot from the second snare, jumped up, and scanned the bushes around me. Someone had to be playing a trick on me. Where were they?

Of course, nobody was there. So I continued on, only rather than scanning the horizon and drinking in the beauty of the Greek countryside as I should have been, my hiking style quickly changed to one of scanning the miniscule details of the trail directly in front of my feet. In no time at all, I had discovered and managed to avoid several more of the near-invisible wire snares placed strategically at the edge of the trail. As the adrenaline died down and I began to relax once more, I realized that these wickedly affective little traps were not targeting me or any other human; they were probably set by the locals to catch rabbits for dinner.

-----

Back in the Tuli Wilderness, we set out up the wash. The sandy bottom was blanketed with the tracks of various African game, and there was a noticeable lack of human footprints. In this truly wild place, the animals ruled, and the humans were only temporary, infrequent visitors.

I took the right-hand side of the wash and we started walking. Within about 5 minutes, I was examining a well-worn game trail that dumped steeply into the drainage when I noticed something that didn't look right.

Two pieces of thick, heavy wire were drawn together in a loop about three feet in diameter, the free end attached firmly to the trunk of a solid tree. The loop itself was suspended from a branch, about six to seven feet off the ground, by a thin strip of bark cut from a mopane tree. This was a big, heavy snare, set in a much higher position than I was expecting after the small snares I had seen in Greece. On the inside of the loop, the two ends of wire were cut sharply and extended about four to six inches out from the snare, turned at a purposeful angle designed to inflict maximum bleeding of the snared animal. It was a brutally simple killing machine.

-----

There's another type of animal trap that has become very popular in wild areas in recent years. Camera traps are frequently used today by programs such as the Botswana Conservation and Research Project. These cameras are set up in remote locations and left for days, sometimes even weeks at a time, and are programmed to either take photographs or short videos when their built-in motion detectors sense any kind of movement in front of the lens. The widespread use of camera

174

traps in effect puts a lot more eyeballs out in the field, enabling observation at more locations, and for 24 hours a day.

"When we were first introduced to camera traps," Andrew told me, "it completely changed the way we did conservation research in the Tuli."

"What's the most interesting thing you've caught on a camera trap?" I asked him, expecting his answer to be about one of the more exotic, rarely seen species of Africa wildlife.

"Well, we caught a poacher once..."

In the very place where we were looking for snares that day, Andrew had set a camera trap more than a year ago. Later, upon reviewing the images of the various animals caught on camera traversing the area, he stumbled across an image of a man. A man he didn't recognize. A man who wasn't supposed to be there. A man who was trespassing, in an area known for poaching, and carrying the tools that a poacher typically carries.

The image of the poacher was of high enough quality that his face was easily identifiable. The photograph was taken to the local tribal elders, who instantly recognized the man as an inhabitant of their village. They said they would take care of the problem. And the man was never seen poaching in the area again.

Tribal law still weighs heavy in the traditional villages of Botswana. When an incident happens, the elders review the evidence presented to them and then pass judgment and decide on the punishment. In some cases, such as poaching, the punishment is a public lashing, and the number of lashes is determined relative to the severity of the crime. Perhaps the most important element of this legal process is the public shaming the perpetrator endures, which turns out to be a much more effective deterrent than those imposed by our traditional western law. And there are no appeals.

After the man caught poaching on camera received his public lashing, a rumor started to spread through the local community about the technology that was used to catch him. The rumor was that the staff of the Tuli Wilderness had installed numerous cameras throughout the bush, all of which were connected via live satellite feed back to the main office where a person sat 24 hours a day monitoring the cameras, ready to pick up their cell phone and call the tribal elders who would dole out immediate punishment. As this rumor spread, poaching plummeted dramatically in the area. Not surprisingly, the staff of the Tuli Wilderness made no attempt to correct this misinformation.

-----

If finding and removing snares is rewarding, not finding them is even better, as it means that the deterrents put in place are having a positive effect. Near the northern border of the Tuli Wilderness, I had found the first snare, and Johannes said it was fresh—it had just been set earlier that very day—so we knew the poachers were once again active in the area. Seconds later, Johannes found a second, smaller snare, much better hidden, only a dozen feet away from where I had found the first one.

We fanned out from this area and eventually found a total of three snares. It was not as many as we were hoping to find, but as Andrew pointed out, each snare you find is one animal saved.

As we widened our net, I veered north, intent on making it all the way to the border fence. I had long heard that one of the unique aspects of the Tuli Wilderness and in fact of the entire Northern Tuli Game Reserve was that it was unfenced; the animals were free to roam over an expansive area, with complete disregard for the arbitrary borders and property boundaries invented by humans. So the first time someone mentioned the northern boundary fence, I was a bit confused.

"So what's up with the northern fence?" I asked Andrew. "I though the Tuli was completely unfenced?"

"The fence isn't around the Tuli," he said. "It's around the village."

"Everywhere else in the world, they put fences around the wildlife to protect the people. Botswana is the only country in the world that puts fences around the people, to protect the wildlife."

"I think Botswana got it right," he added.

The fence was easy to find, and was quite an impressive sight: it was high, with barbed wire around the top, and all vegetation stripped away for 15 to 20 feet on either side for easy patrolling. It reminded me more of a fence you would see at an international border than one protecting a small village from a wilderness area (or vice versa). But, just like an international border fence in a remote area, it was easy to spot the holes in it. As imposing as it was from a distance, you didn't have to get too close to it to see that it looked more like Swiss cheese than an impenetrable barrier.

The ubiquitous holes in and under the fence meant easy access for poachers looking to exploit the plethora of wildlife on our side. These poachers were not the decedents of their ancestors in the traditional sense; they were not the latest breed of nomadic hunter-gatherers, living a traditional lifestyle in tune with their natural surroundings, their lives and the lives of their family entirely dependent on a successful catch. No, these were an entirely different breed of modern, westernized Africans, with jobs, living in a village with modern conveniences. Poaching an Impala or a Kudu was not going to feed their family; it was just a quick and easy way to get some extra money in their pockets.

-----

As we walked through the brush and the trees looking for more snares, Johannes paused and looked down in the middle of an open sandy area between the vegetation.

"Lion," he said.

After a moment or two of closer examination, "Sebatana."

He quickly found another set of tracks next to Sebatana's. It was one of her male cubs, and the tracks were only a day or two old.

"And that's what makes our work here even more important," Andrew said.

The poachers were out here for some antelope meat, which was a quick and easy sell in the bush meat trade. Regardless of the illegality, immorality, and brutality of it all, at least the impala, the kudu, and the other species of African antelope were quite plentiful in the Tuli. But a snare set here could catch a lion just as easily as it could catch an Impala. A dead impala would be a sad thing, but it wouldn't have as devastating an effect on the ecosystem as would a dead lion—especially if that lion was one of Sebatana's cubs, the only known male lions here, representing what may be the last hope for the wild lion population in the Tuli.

A few feet away from the dual lion tracks, Johannes intently studied multiple markings left on a different patch of ground before retelling a story written in the sand earlier that day. It was the tracks of an impala, with a thin, pencil-like line arcing through the sand next to it. Nearby there was also the clear impression of a tennis shoe. This unlucky impala had become caught in a poacher's snare, but somehow managed to break free. As it tried to get away, still tangled in the snare and dragging it behind, it was followed closely by the poacher, no doubt hoping to stumble upon the already dead impala, or at least find it in such a weakened or disabled state that it would be easy to dispatch with his machete. With an expert tracker like Johannes, stories like this easily unfolded before us, all from the reading of a few simple markings in the sand.

We headed back to the vehicle and drove south for about 10 minutes, then stopped. This location, further away from the border fence and deeper in the Tuli Wilderness, also had a history of poaching, and Andrew wanted us to check it out before it got dark.

-----

"The last time I came out here," Andrew said, "I found 70 snares in about an hour." But due to staffing changes, the holiday season, and the floods, there had been a little bit of a lull in the Botswana Conservation and Research Program, and it had been several months since volunteers had fanned out in these areas to actively look for snares.

We had little time before it would be too dark to see anything, so we quickly spread out across the landscape and commenced our search. We found five snares at this location in just about 20 minutes, before Andrew told us that we needed to head back to the vehicle before it got too dark.

A few minutes later, halfway back to the vehicle, in a sandy spot between some rocky outcrops, Andrew noticed a track below him. His brow furrowed, and he looked towards Johannes.

"What the hell is that?" he asked the elder Bushman. It was the second of two times I saw Andrew puzzled by a track.

Johannes looked down. "Dog," he said, immediately followed by "Domestic."

The Tuli Wilderness is no place for a domestic dog. The presence of one could only mean one thing.

"This is a poacher, out hunting with his dog," Andrew said, clearly troubled. "The level of activity has definitely stepped up here. We will be coming back. At least once a week. We need to let the poachers know that we're back."

# Dirt like Blood

There's something so primal about red dirt. At least it's always been that way to me. Whenever I see red dirt, I experience a mysterious attraction.

Soil appears red when it contains a high concentration of iron. Perhaps somewhere, deep in our DNA, our instincts tell us to go towards the blood red dirt because of the iron content. Humans need iron to survive. It's literally in our blood.

Or perhaps it's something else, something more cerebral. Perhaps it's more of a calling; to go back, to a place we've never been, but to the place we came from.

Like the salmon born and raised in captivity, released to the wild, attracted like a magnet to one stream out of so many, a stream it has never been to before, yet it somehow knows: This is it. This is the one. This is home.

Like a magnet, Africa had pulled me back. It was an attraction that was strong, steady, and irresistible; it tugged a little at my brain, and at my heart, but mostly at my gut, rekindling a deep desire—a desire to return to a place I'd never been before, the Tuli Wilderness of Botswana; but to a place where I had always been, through my ancestors, through all of our ancestors, so long ago: Africa.

To finally see a place I've always seen.

To get to know a place I've always known.

To finally understand where I came from. Where we all came from.

The real "old country". The original homeland.

Because we are all African. The rest is just a matter of timing.

-----

I remember once hearing a scientist say that by the time you smell something, microscopic particles of whatever you smell have already entered deep into your body. Although the context was toxic and potentially poisonous chemicals, the same goes for anything else—if you smell it, it has entered your body. By the time you've smelled it, it's already inside of you; it's become part of you.

"Tuli" is the Setswana word for dust, and the dust is everywhere in the Tuli region. It works its way in to everything. You can smell it in your nostrils. You can taste it on your tongue. You can feel the grittiness in your mouth.

It's hard to put an experience like my time in the Tuli Wilderness into words, but I have attempted to do so to the best of my abilities here. It was an experience, or more of a magnificent portfolio of experiences, that will stick with me forever. The Tuli is inside of me. It's become part of me. I can still taste it. It's pumping through my veins.

182

-----

Two weeks, alone but not alone, in a place where man was meant to be—always meant to be. I set about this adventure thinking that it was just a deeply personal journey, maybe even a "midlife crisis," a vacation of sorts meant to reconnect with nature and with the true meaning of humanity. But in the end, it was not about a vacation, but about a life.

It wasn't an escape from technology, civilization, and people, but a blending of old and new experiences, of the past and the future. And though at times it was deeply personal and illuminating, in the end, it wasn't at all about "me"; it was about something bigger.

Going back isn't a destination. It's a journey. A journey that never ends.

Back to the basics.

Back to the beginning.

Back to the bundu.

-----

"All I wanted to do now was get back to Africa. We had not left it yet, but when I would wake in the night, I would lie, listening, homesick for it already."

— Ernest Hemmingway

# Another Shit Day in Africa

Even a short visit to Africa can create a lot of lifetime memories. Events, scenes, and happenings that are spectacular, stunning, fantastic, or unbelievable seem to happen with surprising frequency on this magical continent.

They have a saying down in Africa that they regularly use when confronted with something extraordinary and memorable: "Another shit day in Africa." And most of these "shit day" moments seem to happen around or at sunset, even when the sunset itself isn't that great.

Irony, it seems, is alive and well in Africa.

-----

Driving south on Mohave Highway one evening, tired after a long, hot, exhausting day of road repair, all anyone could think about was getting back to Serolo Camp, eating a quick dinner, taking a shower, and collapsing into bed. We couldn't get back to camp fast enough.

As we approached the edge of Kudu Ridge, where the road follows a natural break known as Elephant Neck through the ridge, one of those special African moments suddenly appeared before us. There, in the fading light, a lone steenbock stood perched on a rocky outcrop, standing at attention at the highest point. In the gloaming, that time after the sun has crept below the horizon but before the last light is completely gone, the

185

animal and the entire landscape were awash with a gentle pink-orange glow.  As I struggled to snap a photograph of this moving scene, Andrew hardly noticed.  He was too busy looking at the body language of the steenbock.

"Predator!" he yelled!  "Lion, leopard, or hyena!"

He slammed on the brakes, jumped out of the vehicle, and took off running towards the rocks where the little steenbock was perched.  It was only then that I realized that Andrew had not actually seen a predator; instead, he knew by observing the body language of the steenbock that it was keyed in on a predator.

I watched in awe as Andrew deftly ran up the side of the cliff.  The steenbock saw him too, and was now more concerned than ever—there was only one easy way up and down that cliff, and Andrew was taking it.  In what it must have seen as a split-second decision literally between a rock and a hard place, the steenbock decided to evacuate its perch and take the only sensible way down.  I watched from the parked vehicle, 100 feet away, and couldn't help laughing at the sight of Andrew and the steenbock running in opposite directions, passing each other only a foot or two apart, the steenbock deathly afraid that this agile human was a predator and was going to attack it.  Meanwhile Andrew was so focused on getting to the top of the outcrop as quickly as possible that he now seemed oblivious to the presence of the steenbock (and I verified with him later that he never even noticed how close he came to it).

As soon as he was on the high point of the ridge, Andrew immediately began scanning the area out in the mopane trees where the steenbock had been keying.  After a minute or two, a look of disappointment washed over his face.  He saw what the steenbock had seen — a tuft of dark fur out in the distance, bobbing up and down between the mopane. It looked an awful lot like the tail of a lion, but it wasn't. "Wildebeest tail," he yelled down to us. "Oh well. The sunset is going to be spectacular from up here. Why don't you come up for a few minutes?"

The rest of us got out of the vehicle and scrambled up the rock. It was the ideal roost for wild animals to do what they are programmed to do — watch for predators or prey, depending on which side of the food chain they were on. It was an equally perfect spot for us civilized animals to do what we seem to be programmed to do — enjoy the scenery.

We stood on top of the rock where the steenbock had been just a few minutes earlier and took it all in. A spectacular vista opened up before us, at first saturated with shades of calming pastels, the contrast gradually increasing before our eyes as the light faded quickly, the landscape taking on a new intensity as it struggled with futility to stay alight for just a moment or two longer.

On the surface, it was just another sunset, one of thousands I had seen and would see in my lifetime. But something made this one of those special moments I would remember for the rest of my life. What made this so special? It's hard to say exactly. A bunch of things happened to come together perfectly, converging at that exact place, at that precise moment in time, turning the ordinary into the extraordinary. You can't predict when magic is going to happen. Just sit back and enjoy the show.

As the sky took on its most vivid colors, a moment or two before the sunset started to fade away and we headed back to the vehicle, Andrew turned to me with a big grin on his face.

"Another shit day in Africa, eh, Matt?"

-----

"You never forget this place."

  —Christoff

Made in the USA
San Bernardino, CA
27 May 2013